Hot Rod Chassis - How To
Understand, Install, Update '28 to '64

Brent VanDervort

Published by:
Wolfgang Publications Inc.
P.O. Box 223
Stillwater, MN 55082
www.wolfpub.com

Legals

First published in 2016 by Wolfgang Publications Inc.,
P.O. Box 223, Stillwater MN 55082

ISBN 13: 978-1-929133-70-3

Printed and bound in U.S.A.

Hot Rod Chassis-How To

Acknowledgements

Tremendously useful technical input was received by the author thru the suppliers listed in that section. Many other fellow hot rodders and racers have also contributed to the growth of my technical knowledge. The staff at my hot rod suspension and chassis business have been a huge help. In particular are Mike Craig, Randy Banks, Jeff Watts, and Tim Tullo.

The experience gained as a State Inspector for the National Street Rod Association was very useful as a great number of hot rods were examined in enough detail so that many lessons were learned about both the right and wrong ways to build a hot rod. The Goodguys Rod & Custom Association enabled much growth by their allowing me a forum through a monthly Tech column in their Gazette publication. Writing that column put me in a position to research topics in depth in order to speak accurately while passing learned information along to the readers.

On the publishing side, I have been fortunate to work with Tim Remus and Jacki Mitchell at Wolfgang Publishing. Bill Longyard has also written for that group and has contributed photos and valuable advice to this project. These fine professionals have been of great assistance in assembling and editing a book which we all hope will prove to be of real value to the hot rodding public. Behind every person is another supportive person, in this case my wife Deborah. Her patient tolerance and support of my hot rod habit has been essential in providing the time and freedom to explore the world of hot rodding.

Sources

The list of suppliers below have proven themselves to be superb sources of quality hot rod suspension components. Perhaps even more importantly, their unselfish availability to answer and resolve technical questions is unparalleled in the industry.

Addco.com	sway bars
Borgeson.com	steering components
Carolinaswaybar.com	sway bars
ChassisEngineeringInc.com	hot rod suspension and chassis
EatonDetroitSpring.com	replacement leaf and coil springs
ECI hotrodbrakes@sbcglobal.net	brake kits, pedal assemblies
Fatman Fabrication Fatmanfab.com	hot rod suspension and chassis
Hellwigproducts.com	sway bars
Ididitinc.com	steering columns and parts
Monroeshocks.com	shock absorbers
PeteandJakes.com	hot rod suspension and chassis
QA-1.net	coilovers, shocks and suspension kits
Ridetech.com	airride, shocks, coilovers and suspension kits
Independent chassis hotrodit.com	hot rod suspension and chassis
Wilwood.com	upgraded brake kits, pedal assemblies

Introduction

The inspiration for this book came from the earlier book entitled "Building Hot Rods". That earlier volume is a compilation of some of the more useful Tech columns that I had written for the *Goodguys Gazette* over a 20 year period. Conversations with readers of that book made it clear that they were hungry for more in depth Tech info aimed specifically at Suspension related topics. And so this book came to be, with all newly written material, photos, and illustrations.

The goal is to present technical info in a way that is clear and uncomplicated. It is the opinion of many that a topic which is well understood can always be reduced to some basic truths that can be communicated with plain language and simple analogies. There are times when in depth engineering based writing is of great value, but when a topic can only be explained with the use of higher mathematics and complex illustrations, perhaps that subject isn't really understood as well as claimed. Better understanding seems to lead to those basic truths that can be used in the real world by real rodders.

We hope to present facts based on science and physics that the hot rodder will find of interest, and that will assist him in the building and improvement of his project. As we improve the horsepower related performance of our vehicles, we should also improve safety and comfort through better braking, cornering, and suspension capability. We humbly hope to contribute to that positive evolution thru the topics discussed in this book.

Brent's first book is a collection of two decades worth of tech articles written for The Goodguys Gazette - available from Fatman.

Brent, long time owner of Fatman Fabrications, answering questions while working the Fatman booth at Back to the 50s in St. Paul, MN.

Chapter One

Start with a good Foundation

The Bricks and Mortar

Any discussion of the design and fabrication of automotive suspension has to start with a thorough understanding of frame design. We'll include a later discussion of unibody cars, which use their unique body sheet-metal design for the same purpose as a vehicle with a separate body and frame. Since the frame provides mounting points for the suspension along with the body, it provides the very foundation upon which the entire vehicle is constructed.

It is critical that the frame be extremely rigid for suspension designs to work as expected. Any flex will have the effect of altering the suspension mounting points which are so elemental to the anticipated geometry. When we later reach a discussion of actual suspension design it will be very

A really nice hot rod build always begins with a good foundation. Proper stance and attention to detail will get your own project the notice it deserves.

The X member design featured in this new chassis for a 1940 Chevy exhibits far more torsional rigidity than the original frame, which had just 4 simple crossmembers. Combined with 3/16" wall main rails, this hot rod will perform and ride far better than a modified original.

clear that the suspension must handle the irregularities of the road and body roll rather than having the frame perform that function. For now we can take a look at the history of automotive frame designs so that their evolution will help us see how to design a very rigid chassis.

With the early auto frames being of open construction they were very prone to twisting. As one can imagine, broken frames were a common occurrence.

One of the unique features of the Ford Model T and later Model A were that they were made with steel far superior to the steel used by most other makes. The story goes that Henry Ford, who always

This stock '28-'31 Model a Ford chassis exhibits the open ladder style chassis.

Note that this complete '35 to '40 Ford frame with Mustang II IFS installation includes a tubular engine mount that carries the weight of the engine to the crossmember rather than merely to the frame rail, which prevents frame twisting.

The narrower truck chassis like the '53-'56 Ford PU will not deflect as much as a wider chassis so the need for a complex X member is minimal. With a width of merely 34" combined with 6 crossmembers and 2" x 5" x .188" wall main rails, very little twist will ever be seen, while the more open design provides much easier fitting of the exhaust system.

had an interest in racing, was at a race in France. After witnessing a wreck involving a Mors car he was impressed by how well the frame had held together. We know that steel today as chrome moly. Chrome moly has a far higher tensile strength than more common SAE 1020 carbon steel.

Although it's also more expensive than mild steel, Henry used this superior steel to build frames that were far stronger than most and could accept extremely rough use, the result of driving on the terrible roads of the time.

Steel that could twist without fatiguing and cracking was combined with riveted rather than welded joints so that the frame could absorb some of the punishment beyond the ability of the suspension.

That very desirable higher tensile strength does create a problem when those original Model T and A frames are used modern hot rods.

Chrome moly can certainly be welded, but special procedures must be followed. It should be preheated before welding, and post heated too - to relieve residual stresses. It has a rate of thermal expansion far different from that of ordinary mild steel so welding the two together creates many problems.

I have personally witnessed a welded seam continue to crack right behind a progressing weld when mild steel was used to box the frame. Sure, many Model A and T frames have been successfully welded and held up just fine, but these cars are particularly good candidates for a complete new frame made with mild steel.

As simple as these frames are, new frames are very affordable compared to the effort, expense, and risk of modifying the originals. Since non-Ford, and 1932-up Ford frames are made with mild steel there is no reason whatsoever that these original frames cannot be properly modified and used for a modern hot rod.

In the early 1930s manufacturers had to deal with better roads and more power. Chevrolet went in the direction of what was basically a ladder frame, but made with a fully boxed rail right from the factory.

This light weight yet stronger frame first appeared on the '36 Chevy Standard car, and was manufactured by forming 14 gauge (approximately .081" thick) into a top hat shape and then spot welding a similar thickness flat plate to the bottom.

This style frame worked out well enough that it was adopted for all '37-'54 Chevy cars, and was seen on some later Studebakers and Willys light truck chassis. These frames have proven to perform well with modern suspensions and drivetrains but require different and special techniques when modified. We'll get into those concepts in our next chapter.

In order to provide the torsional rigidity required for a more quiet and longer lasting car, X-member construction became popular.

Larger cars such as the Packards had these frames from the early thirties while Ford added this design for the '34-'48 years with GM adopting it for their premium lines such as the Chevy Master, '34-'36 and '34-up Buick, Olds, Pontiac and Cadillac.

The engineering concept is to achieve torsional rigidity with an X-shaped central structure that feeds road following stresses from any corner into the center of the X. Thus the other X-member legs and rails are able to assist in resisting frame twist.

A curious twist (pardon the pun) on this design was the '58-'64 GM cars which retained the X-member while doing away with the side rails in the center section of the chassis. Although this design certainly proved adequate in normal ser-

A well-designed chassis modification preserves the integrity of the X-member while providing extra space for a modern automatic transmission.

The 1968 Mustang displays the frameless unibody construction that became popular with all manufacturers in the '60s especially for their compact and sporty cars.

9

vice, there have been concerns about hard use and the ability to resist side impact in a collision. Today's hot rod chassis use both structures for maximum frame rigidity.

As shown in the nearby photo of the '48 Ford chassis, it is often helpful to open up the center of the X-member to make room for modern automatic transmissions that are larger than the original manual trans.

This type chassis has become highly favored in terms of strength but will require special attention when it comes to mounting modern suspension and particularly the exhaust system.

Strangely enough, most manufacturers went back to a more open style frame in the post WWII era. Heavier gauge steel was used to regain some rigidity while many convertibles and some of the new hardtop body designs were fitted with additional bracing that often included an X-member. Since the more open non-post sedan cars

have much less inherent rigidity, these modifications were necessary.

When an X-member was not added, cracks in the rear quarter at the window line are often seen, a common problem on '55-57 Chevy and '55-56 Ford hardtops.

As stock car racing became popular these frame options were used to advantage. Drag racers wanted as little weight as possible so tended to use post sedans and the more simple open frames. Oval track racers often had to make a minimum weight by rule and nearly always chose a stronger X-member convertible frame for that reason.

The unibody construction era was pioneered by the late 1940s Hudson and Nash cars. Weight savings are crucial to enhancing performance and economy. The heavy full frame is eliminated in favor of a technique where the car-body sheet-metal structure provides enough rigidity that a frame becomes unnecessary, mounting points for

The coil-over unitized spring and shock seen at each corner of this '47-'54 Chevy PU chassis will provide superb ride and handling. Their use does require special attention to the frame mounting to handle the localized stresses which are completely different than those on the original front and rear parallel leaf spring suspension.

the suspension and drivetrain are part of the design.

This type construction was actually pioneered by European cars such as the Citroen Traction Avant and also in airplane construction.

As the U.S. retooled from car to airplane production during WWII, there was a tremendous transfer of technology back to the automotive industry.

Many areas of the country such as the Los Angeles basin, the Upper Midwest and Long Island N.Y. had a prominent place in the aeronautical industry which figured heavily in the growth of local hot rodding. Good examples of the technology transfer include high compression engines, high octane fuel, supercharging and stressed skin construction. It's easy to see that experience gained building bombers could be brought back into the auto culture

As the sixties came along, fuel economy again became a priority and new unibody cars like the Falcon, Nova and Valiant were born. After a few years and some inspired marketing by designers at the Ford Motor Company, these cars were powered up with V-8 engines and sporty bodywork on what were essentially economy-car platforms. By combining light, economy car structures with V-8 engines, Detroit gave birth to the Ponycar era. Again, both economy and performance could be enhanced by the weight savings delivered by the frameless unibody structures.

An unusual variation on the unibody theme was the Camaro and Second Generation Nova. A half frame, or subframe was attached to the unibody in a way that supported the front suspension and drivetrain. That provided a more solid structure which could better withstand greater engine power and handling stresses.

The preceding is a general discussion of the various methods of providing a chassis that can be rigid enough to allow the car to function as designed. With that foundation we can now go on to explore the ways to upgrade each type of construction, along with both the similar and different techniques that each type requires to function best.

But first, the builder needs to decide: should the original chassis be preserved and modified, or would they be better served with an entirely new structure?

The X-member seen in this '55-'57 frame from the aftermarket makes for a frame that is much stronger than stock.

Boxing A Stock Chassis

The entire purpose of frame boxing is to convert an open channel to a much stronger closed rectangle shape. To visualize that transformation, take hold of a common cardboard shoebox. Notice that the open, lidless lower box is extremely flexible. Then add the equally flimsy lid and that complete box becomes amazing rigid. That rigidity added by completing the entire box shape is exactly what we need in a hot rod with improved power and suspension. If the frame moves before the suspension does, that suspension simply cannot perform as expected. Boxing also provides a convenient and reinforced point to which extra crossmembers and mounts for engines, etc can be located.

2. Clamp the boxing plate blank in place to begin the marking process.

1. A large adjustable wrench is an ideal tool to straighten the frame flanges prior to boxing.

3. The frame outside shape can be marked with a scribe or a Sharpie pen as it will be easier to see the line.

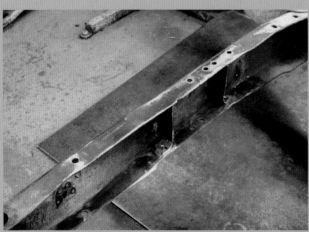

1.5. That nice straight frame flange has prepared the frame for a really professional appearing boxing job.

3.5. Some fabricators prefer to mark the frame shape with a light coat of cheap aerosol spray paint.

Boxing A Stock Chassis

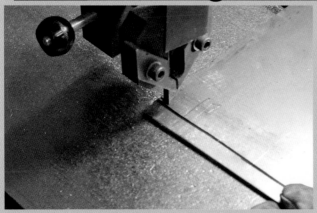

4. Make your cut about 1/8" INSIDE your marked line to allow space for the weld to be made and remain intact after final grinding.

6. After making sure the boxing plate fits correctly, we tack weld the plate in place. Remember to weld in 2-3" sections, skipping from place to place, top to bottom and side to side.

4.5. The plate used here is 6X.125".

7. Close up shows how a gap was left for the bead, especially at the top.

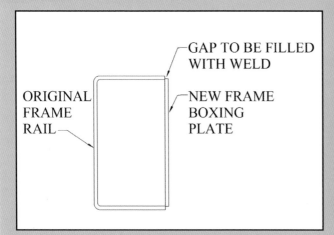

5. This diagram shows how the ideal dimension leaves the boxing plate just a little smaller than flush, which creates a void where the weld bead will be.

8. Here's the very neat and finished installation.

Chapter Two

Terms

Let's get 'em Right

Now that you have decided to build a hot rod, you'll do well to know something about suspension. It's important enough when you choose to purchase a new chassis, where you are buying the builder's knowledge and experience and trusting in his proper design and fabrication of that chassis. On the other hand if you are going to modify your own chassis through the use of available kits or even your own design, understanding suspension design becomes even more critical.

Before you can build a chassis from scratch, or modify an existing chassis, you really need to understand the basics of suspension design and operation.

Your knowledge will need to be very deep if you are so bold as to design your own suspension. If you choose the more likely path of installing commercially available suspension kits you need still should understand enough of the engineering so that you can choose the type of suspension that is best for your needs. The type of spring, steering, brakes, and other details will be important. Your budget and the level of build you pursue will also be factors in your choices.

Hopefully, after reading this book you will also be able to recognize good sound design practices from others that may be less desirable. A particular chassis design may elevate the perception of quality in the parts you choose through high levels of intricacy and shine. However, fancy ads and beautiful workmanship will not compensate for poor engineering. The laws of physics and geometry have not changed since the ancient Greeks explored them, nor are they affected by the use of CAD drafting or sophisticated manufacturing. Good design never goes out of style. Pure and simple, the primary function of your suspension is to maximize the contact patch of your tires in order to provide performance and safety. This book is an attempt to help you learn enough to be able to see the differences in design and recognize which will work best on your project.

In the course of my career in hot rod suspension design I have had the privilege to present a monthly column in the Goodguys Gazette and present seminars at their events and hot rod industry trade shows. Before we get into a discussion of all the facets of hot rod chassis and suspension design it

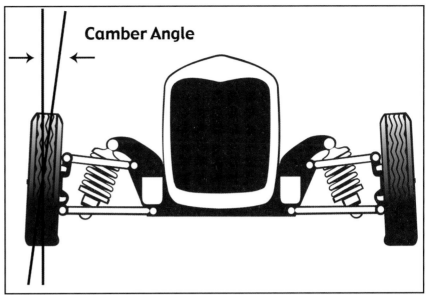

Any understanding of how suspension functions has to begin with a clear idea of what toe in, camber and caster look like and are adjusted. Then one can go on to see how manipulating those three properties allows the designer to get the needed handling characteristics.
Eric Aurand

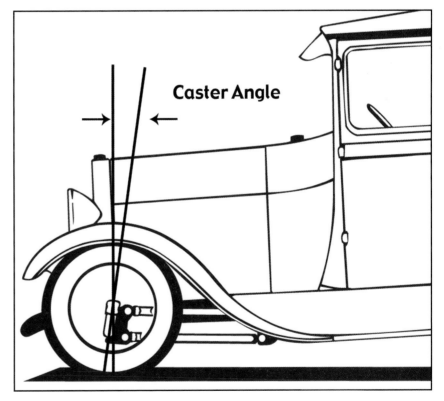

Above: Camber is the angle of the tire. tipped in as shown is negative while tipped out is positive. Caster is the cangle of the kingpin or center line running through the two ball joints. Tipped back as shown is positive, tipped forward it negative.
Eric Aurand

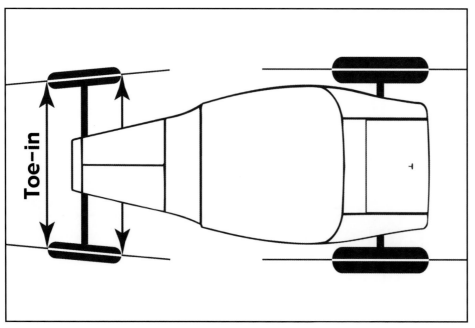

As shown, toe-in is the difference between the measurement taken at the rear of the tires as compared to that taken at the front.

huge differences of opinion which we won't deal with here. We are concerned with street driven cars that may see occasional Autocross use. What we desire is a car that goes where you steer when you steer it without argument. You will almost not notice the suspension when it is working correctly. If you are constantly correcting for how the chassis tracks in the road, something is wrong! The avoidance of that chassis having a mind of it's own is what we are striving for. Alignment settings are critical to allowing a good design to work correctly. One can have the best guitar made but when it is not properly tuned, it will sound terrible. Alignment is the final tuning of a suspension system.

Eric Aurand

will be important to define and explain some of the basic terms. That will be of great help as we discuss those variations in design. If a particular topic seems confusing as discussed you may find it helpful to refer to this Chapter Two - Terms.

BASIC ALIGNMENT

This can be a huge subject all its own. Racers in different venues such as oval track and road racing will have specific settings which are used to emphasize a particular characteristic of their track set up. That is an entirely different subject with

Toe in is likely the most basic alignment setting as it is adjustable on even the most elementary solid axle suspensions. For stability, rear wheel driven cars will be set around 1/8" toe in. You would think that zero toe in would be ideal and that is correct. However, in the real world there is always some "slop" or play in the various steering components. A few thousandths of an inch tolerance in the four tie rods, the idler am, the steering box etc can total up to a significant amount of play. By setting static toe in (sitting still but fully loaded) that play will be compensated for as normal road forces push the tires back and take up that play. (Front wheel drive cars use a little toe out for a similar purpose as the wheels are pulled forward).

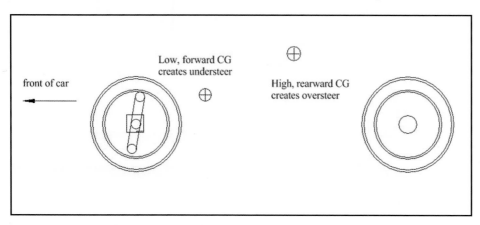

All in all it's a matter of where the car's center of gravity (CG) is located. The higher the CG the more you need anti sway bars, and the end of the car nearest the CG will tend to need more help.

Camber is generally held at 0 to 1 degree positive, which puts the top of the tire outboard from the bottom. This creates a tendency for the tires to turn in toward the vehicle centerline, providing straight-line stability. This works on trailers too, which have positive camber when new and negative camber after being overloaded. This negative camber creates a wandering tendency that can be corrected by bending the center of the axle upward. That wandering tendency is exactly why highway use tends to positive camber while Autocross drivers would prefer negative camber.

Caster is where it gets interesting! By leaning the kingpin angle (or a line thru the ball joint pivots) back somewhat, an effect is created where turning the wheels raises the car. Therefore, the car's own weight attempts to push the wheels straight again. As you can imagine, more caster provides increased straight-line stability at the expense of harder steering. Bonneville cars often run up to 15 degrees positive caster to gain the required stability. Straight axle suspensions typically call for 4-6 degrees positive caster. The addi-

tional caster helps prevent the wandering and shimmy that can occur on straight axles. Since our modern tires are shorter diameter than the originals, running caster to the strong side of the range works well. These suspensions usually end up under relatively light cars, so the extra steering effort shouldn't be a problem.

The earliest cars with factory independent front suspensions often call for zero, or even negative caster, with the top of the kingpin angle forward. The intent was apparently easier steering, with stability less of an issue with the tires and roads of 50 years ago. We recommend 1-2 degrees positive caster for better road manners without appreciable steering difficulty.

The immensely popular Mustang II suspensions with power rack and pinion steering have a tendency toward excessively light and quick steering. The original '74'-78 MII racks were the culprit as they were designed to run at only 600-800 psi, much lower than common power-steering pumps. The better kits now are made to accept the later '79 - '93 Mustang power racks, which are

Bumpsteer

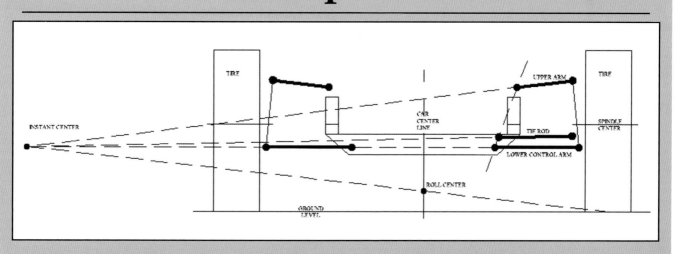

Bumpsteer is an uncommanded (not initiated by the driver) change in the direction of the tire as the suspension reacts to the road. It is NOT a vibration in the wheel, but rather is often felt as a change in the car's direction as it goes through a bump or encounters body roll. It can affect one wheel or both according to how the chassis is moving, but the net effect will always be a change in the static toe-in setting. This feature can actually be designed in for oval track racing but for cars that need to turn both left and right it will hamper handling and lead to a car that feels very "nervous" on the road. We will be discussing in future sections how it affects all types of suspension, front and rear, and how it can be prevented.

less sensitive thanks to redesign of internal components. These have a nice feel, and seldom require altering line pressure since they were built to better match the normal 1000-1200 psi output of most common power-steering pumps. With either the early or late Mustang power racks, try four degrees positive caster to "tame" the rack by adding to the rack's preference to track straight ahead.

These terms get thrown about rather loosely when handling is discussed. Understeer is the tendency for the car to continue straight ahead rather than follow the direction the driver is steering. In NASCAR parlance it's called "push". Nose heavy cars suffer particularly from under steer, the heavier the engine the more understeer there tends to be. Muscle cars with big blocks are particular victims of this and so require massive antisway bars in front, with heavy springs and shocks to control it. Ride quality often is poor due to such a stiff suspension.

Oversteer is the tendency for the rear of the car to slide outboard in the turn, thus tightening the intended turning radius. Racers and TV announcers will often describe this as "being loose". Older cars from the 30s to the 50s often exhibit this tendency as they have a relatively high center of gravity and the car's weight will be carried close to even, front-to-back. In this case, rear sway bars are required more than in front.

THE KEY TO GEOMETRY

There is one central concept to understanding nearly any automotive geometry question. Whether you're dealing with valve trains, throttle or shift linkage, or suspension, you must first clearly understand Arc Length Theory.

When a control link moves, it swings in an arc, whose radius is dictated by its length from the pivot point to the end in motion. As it swings it changes the effective length due to that natural radius, Depending on how the mounting points relate to each other, that length change can be equal in either direction, or longer one way and shorter the other. That's how independent suspension can be designed to lean the tires into the corner for better handling. Manipulating the change in length, the pivot points, and how the links relate to each other, are how we can control the motion of the parts mounted on those links.

Notice in the drawing that when the arm length doubles and the amount of vertical travel remains the same, the angle of rotation for the longer arm is half that of the short arm. Further, the side-to-side effective length displacement of the short arm is twice that of the long arm.

An application of that theory would be hood hinges which on most cars are actually a four bar system. A similar change occurs when hood hinges get bent. When a hood hinge has been sprung the bending of the links

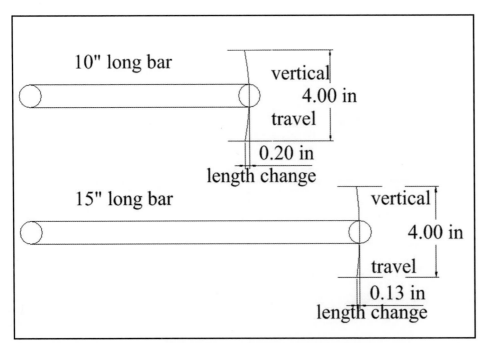

One reason suspension geometry changes with the length of the A arms, tie rod assemblies, rack and pinion dimensions and their pivot locations is that the net horizontal displacement of those links changes with vertical suspension travel. If not properly designed and coordinated, those changes lead to bumpsteer and poor camber control.

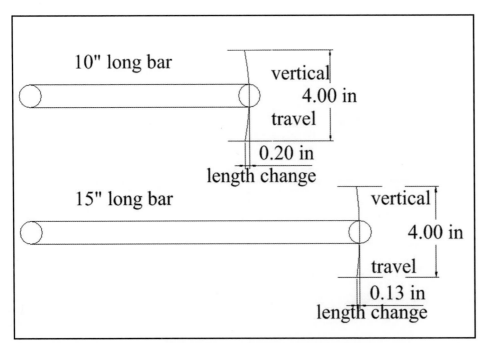

Figure labels: 10" long bar, vertical 4.00 in travel, 0.20 in length change, 15" long bar, vertical 4.00 in travel, 0.13 in length change

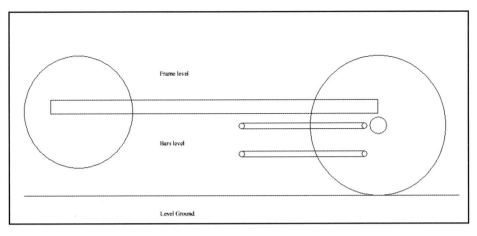

Although well intentioned, setting the chassis level during the build can lead to geometry problems later.

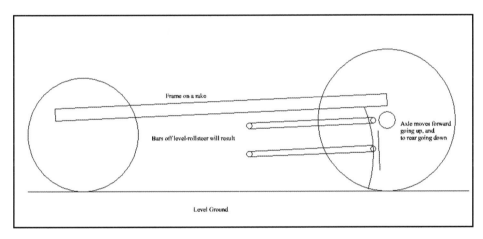

Rollsteer is created here since the previously set up level bars are now angled due to normal chassis rake.

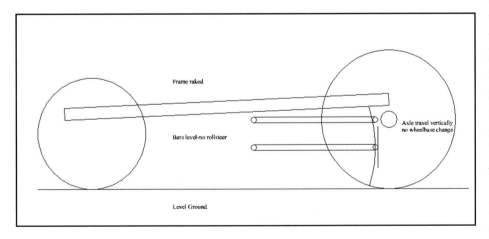

Now we see that setting the chassis on an estimated rake and then levelling the bars will lead to a better handling car.

changes their effective length. The hood no longer is controlled as the designer intended and the hood doesn't fit the opening as it should. That change in the control of a moving object's path is what a designer uses to get the effect he wants, whether for a hood or suspension. Used incorrectly, poor control of the coordination of suspension links will lead to bumpsteer and other forms of bad geometry. Another easy-to-see example of this linkage length change is in rear four-bar suspension. If the bars (links) are level, the up and down motion of the rear end actually causes the rear end to move forward slightly, equally on both sides. (which is why driveshafts have slip joints) The wheelbase gets slightly shorter, but handling is unaffected since the axle remains square in the chassis. It is critical to understand that we refer to true level, with respect to the ground. The angle of the bars with respect to the frame is not important. Let's first look at a rear four-bar that was set up with the frame level from front to back and the bars also level with respect to the ground.

Now we'll see what happens in the real world. Since finished cars seldom sit level front to back, a problem has been created. As the suspension works, the

This roadster is equipped with a high end IFS (Independent Front Suspension) that will work very well. If you are considering buying such a car or simply checking how your own is working, run your hands over the tires. And poor geometry or bad alignment settings will produce a tire wear pattern that has uneven wear, often seen as wedge shaped tread blocks or excessive wear on a particular section of the tire. A suspension that is right will produce a very smooth and even wear pattern that only feels rough when rubbed against the direction of rotation.

wheelbase gets longer on compression and shorter on extension. That's not too bad until we get into a turn and the chassis leans. As the body rolls to the outside, the inner wheel goes down and the outer wheel goes up in relation to

The bars are no longer level with respect to the ground. Based on a left hand turn with the

body and chassis rolling outboard, the inboard side of the rear axle will move forward as the axle moves away from the frame. At the same time the outer end of the axle moves nearer the frame and thus extends the wheelbase. The effect may be very small, perhaps only 1/8" but the combination of axle position is double and our axle is now 1/4" out of square in the chassis.

You would never install an axle that far out of square since you know it will steer to the left at all times. Oversteer has been created. What is happening is referred to as rollsteer since it is forced by body roll moving the suspension link positions while the tires try to remain on the ground. This is one of the reasons the finished chassis rake should be estimated, and set on jack stands at the angle before setting up your suspension. Setting the chassis level front to back is usually dead wrong!

Finally, let's look at an example where we have all the angles right. Experience has shown that a 2-3 degree forward rake is a pretty good average so we'll set the frame that way. Then we set the bars level to the ground. Now the axle moves back and forth as is normal but it remains square in the chassis at all times. Handling is predictable and normal. There is no need to install a monster sway bar to control body roll/rollsteer so ride and handling are enhanced

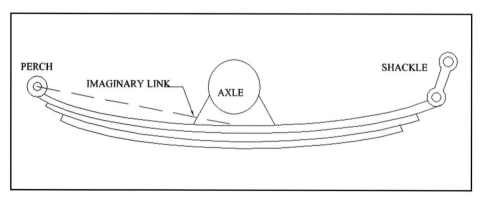

The effective suspension link with a leaf spring connects the solid perch eye to the point where the spring meets the axle mount.

20

rather than being locked up by excessively stiff suspension caused by that overly stiff rear sway bar.

You may have noticed that rods with leaf spring rears also move the axle forward as the car is jacked up and the wheels go down. When a line is drawn through the front perch bolt and the base of the axle saddle, it's apparent that the front half of the spring acts just like a four bar link, and has the same roll steer problem. Lowering blocks raise the rear to lower the car but since the contact point of the spring and lowering block remain the rear pivot point, the imaginary link angle is steep as in our earlier non level 4 bar example so the axle movement fore and aft is exaggerated and roll steer results. De-arched springs are preferable, and help the handling by raising the rear axle while leveling the control link and minimizing rollsteer. It's not a big deal with lowering blocks 2" tall or less but taller blocks create more roll-steer.

As you can imagine, rear sway bars are critical to minimizing this problem. Since the roll steer is created by chassis roll, a higher center of gravity is a great problem. That's why sedans, coupes, and panels need rear sway bars while pickups do fine with none. If your hot rod gets twitchy in a corner, this roll-steer phenomenon is often at fault. You can often get the bars level by raising the axle in the chassis. Try raising the rear end with a taller tire to maintain the original ride height. Sometimes it's easier to alter the height of the pivot points. The key is to maintain level control links.

CORRECT ACKERMAN GEOMETRY FOR FRONT SUSPENSION

When front suspension design is discussed, the Ackerman principle seems to inevitably come up. There appears to be some confusion as to how proper Ackerman is designed into a system, and the effect that improper design has on the suspension function.

Ackerman principle involves manipulating how the front tire's toe in changes when the wheels are rotated to turn the car's direction. We have seen improper use of this principle creating problems on some factory designs, and on hot rods with modified IFS (Independent Front Suspension) and lately with suicide perch straight axles on nostalgia-themed rods.

This Ackerman guy was an Austrian carriage designer from the 1700's, who had a problem with the lightweight wheels of his sporting carriages folding up under heavy use. He realized that the excess stress on the wheels was generated when the wheels did not track smoothly thru the turn. First one wheel, then the other had to slide sideways to "keep up" with the path of the vehicle. He found that the commonly used simple pivoting axle didn't work just right, because the inner wheel has to turn tighter, or toe-out, in order to track properly

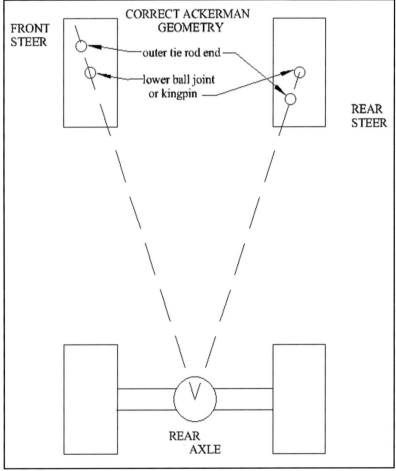

Follow this layout to properly locate your outer tie rod end for front or rear steer, IFS or axle suspensions.

21

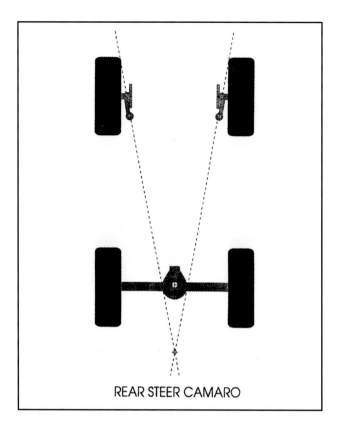

REAR STEER CAMARO

The rear steer Camaro has the best Ackerman of the '67-'81 cars.

in a turn. That necessary toe-out in a turn became the focus of his efforts.

Mr. Ackerman's research showed him that a more complex linkage using tie rods, and pivoting spindles with specially designed steering was necessary. The outer tie rod end pivot must lie on a line passing thru the center of the rear end and the kingpin (lower ball joint on an IFS). That means a front-steered system requires the tie rod pivot to be outboard of the lower ball joint, and inboard for rear-steer system.

Some designs violate this concept, compromising the tire contact patch by creating toe-in during a turn, causing loss of traction. Since the effect is greatest at extreme turn angles, skinny tires mask the effect while fat tires magnify the problem. Hot rodders get in trouble when we decide to swap steering arms to relocate the steering, such as normally rear steered Corvairs with front steer Pinto racks or rear steered Mustang II.

This often occurs with nostalgia rods and T-buckets with early Ford spindles converted to a front tie rod, as is often used with a suicide perch mounting system.

By swapping the spindles side from side and placing the tie rod in front, the suicide perch design allows the car to sit lower, avoiding the rear steer system problem where the tie rod interferes with the frame rail bottom, and often the radius rods as well. You'll find that these cars often exhibit a lot of tire scrub in a turn, and understeer badly due to that constant skidding of one tire or another. Harking back to Mr. Ackerman's problem with folding up front wheels, the early T buckets with skinny wire wheels often failed the same way. Stronger wheels, and wire wheels with a wider hub for better spoke triangulation helped. Even better, Total Performance, being one of the T bucket design leaders, redesigned their steering arms to greatly reduce this problem.

Although it's probably not possible to com-

FRONT STEER CAMARO

The '70-'81 Camaro and '64-'77 Chevelles have reversed Ackerman which results in tire scrub and understeer when turned tightly.

pletely correct the Ackerman with commonly used spindles on straight axles, you can improve the situation greatly with a little work. Since most common axle spindles are forged, their steering arms can be heated and bent to get the outer tie rod end as far out as possible, without interfering with the wheels. You will be pleasantly surprised at how such a small change will improve the car's handling.

We see this reversed Ackerman geometry causing trouble in some factory cars, notably the '64-'77 Chevelle and the '78-'87 G-body Monte Carlo/Malibu/S-10 suspensions. When pushed hard, these cars display pretty serious understeer due to the reversed Ackerman causing a loss of turning traction, as well as a very poor camber curve due to the too-short spindle height and improperly angled upper control arm. These are all front-steer, and the designers had to limit how far outboard the outer tie rod end could be located and still clear the wheel. If your wheel and brake combination allows the space to heat and bend the steering arm outward as discussed earlier, you will be making a worthwhile improvement.

I was surprised to see that many Indy car chassis and some NASCAR designs exhibit reversed Ackerman. A suspension expert on A.J. Foyt's team explained to me that since steering angles were so small during normal racing that the reversed Ackerman presented less a problem than the spindle and shorter A arm design that would have been required for correct Ackerman. Further, I found that the NASCAR short track designs, where steering angles tend to be much greater, use a different design, since the performance requirements and relative importance of geometry features are different. In other words, those race-car designers were faced with the same necessary space and design compromises made by the OEM designers and hot rodders working at home.

A study of the first Ackerman drawing should suggest to you that wheelbase and track width have an effect on the ideal position of the outer tie rod end, and that is exactly true. It is also true that incorrect Ackerman will be increasingly noticed as the angle of a turn increases and that it has little

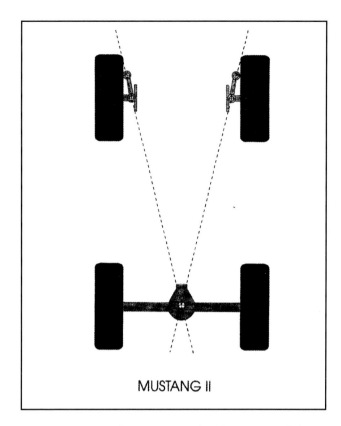

Mustang II IFS have very good Ackerman and therefore handle quite well, especially as they normally exhibit no bumpsteer and have excellent camber control.

effect in small turn angles. Since a great many factory cars exhibit reversed Ackerman it becomes clear that although correct Ackerman will always be preferred, circumstances such as control arm length, wheel offset, differing track width and wheelbase will sometimes make it difficult to achieve. The lesson is that if you must cheat on one aspect of suspension design, Ackerman is a place where you can get away with it. So, you can indeed drive a car with reversed Ackerman, but it will not handle as well or be as safe in an emergency maneuver as one with correct Ackerman. Getting it close to perfect will generally be OK, but get it right if you can for best results.

Chapter Three

Solid Axle Front Suspension

Old Skool is still Cool

The solid axle suspension design goes back as far as the earliest wheeled carts. The classic appeal of an axle on a fenderless car or one with open style fenders is undeniable. Nostalgia buffs would have nothing else on an early rod. The design is easy to understand and install, and orig-

inal axle suspensions found in many cars and trucks can be upgraded to provide decent service. Independent front suspensions (IFS) have become very popular, but many rodders still prefer the elegant simplicity of an axle in their hot rods. The Nostalgia trend, and the so-called rat

When it comes to nostalgia and style, it's hard to beat a dropped axle on an early hot rod!

rod revolution have revived interest in the axle as a viable suspension choice which looks good and can approach the ride and handling qualities of IFS when set up properly. Like anything on a hot rod, the setup is critical to success.

You may be surprised to find that this relatively unsophisticated design is capable of amazing performance in terms of ride and handling when properly

Henry's original buggy sprung front axle with triangular wishbone did an admirable job for years and years. Simple and durable.

arranged. Since the essential design is quite simple it requires and responds to the finer points of component choice and tuning, while an independent front suspension (IFS) is much more forgiving in terms of the final set up. Evidence of that can be seen in oval track racing as well as hot rodding. When shock absorbers and springs provide proper travel and control a solid-axle suspension can perform very well indeed.

What you do get with straight-axle suspension is basic simplicity and a clean appearance, especially with an open wheel rod. Many cars easily accept a modified axle with a minimum of work. Model T's in particular lack enough fender coverage to do a good job of concealing an IFS.

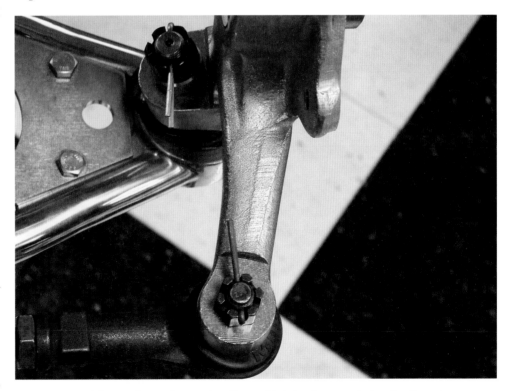

You can readily see the wide parting line which is characteristic of a forged part.

Cast parts exhibit a narrow parting line where the two halves of the mold come together.

We will discuss in detail the types of axle construction and which is best for a particular use later on when we discuss the various radius rods that are used to position them in the chassis. For now let's look at the general construction of those axles.

The most basic of axle types is the good old original forged I-beam. This will be the axle with the highest ultimate strength, but also the heaviest if that matters to you. Dropped versions are available for many cars and trucks, in both modified stock axles and new aftermarket forgings. Some axles are also available in a cast malleable iron, which is nearly as strong as a forging, and well within the necessary safety limits for any normal use. By the way, you can distinguish a forging by a wide parting band on its edge, rather than the narrow parting line common to a casting. Forged axles can be readily welded by the TIG process to attach shock brackets or whatever, but cast axles require very special techniques which are probably best avoided by all but the most knowledgeable welders. Most of the round tube axles we see are made using a tube center section welded to either cast or forged ends. They are jig welded for proper alignment, and really should not have the welds ground down for smoother paint or chrome treatment. The reduction of weld area available to resist stress can create a weak spot, and failures are not unheard of. Some of the first fabbed tube axles from the '70-'85 era had cast ends welded in place. When the welds were ground down, failures did occur. Since modern axles will have forged ends, they are much more reliable, but if your axle has the narrow parting line common to a casting, be cautious about continuing to use it. In fact, chrome plating of high

If you vary the style (paint vs. chrome) and technical options (drum vs. disc brakes), a very individualized suspension can be built. A very basic, but stock rebuilt, un-dropped, drum brake suspension can be an inexpensive first step for a beginning rodder. More upgrades can be added later as your experience, goals, and budget grow.

What you don't get is related directly to the limitations imposed by an axle's need to have each front wheel react to any road surface contacted by the other side, rather than remaining independent as in an IFS. Your ride and handling are unavoidably affected. This effect can be minimized through improvements we'll discuss later. You will often want to add power steering and disc brakes. If taken to the highest style and technical levels, you'll easily spend as much on improvements as you would with most IFS systems. Handling on really rough roads will not be ideal, and the separation strips on concrete highways will be felt. You won't get all the ride and handling advantages of IFS, but it will sure look good!

carbon metals, such as castings, can weaken the axle by a phenomenon known as Hydrogen embrittlement. Molecules of Hydrogen infiltrate the metal's crystalline structure, causing the same effect as a crack. A forged end is not high carbon and thus will not be susceptible to this phenomenon. If your chrome plater looks at you sideways when you ask about this, be very concerned.

Fabricated tube axles are made entirely with seamless, heavy-wall tubing, which is TIG welded. They generally need all their associated brackets welded on, with any normal process being acceptable. Some attempt to mimic the curved shaped common to the axles discussed above, but some have a single bend on each end with a straight center section. That type looks especially good on Model T's with their square radiators and angular fender lines. It is very easy to sleeve and weld them in the center straight sections in order to perfectly dial in their width to properly place a tire under a fender. I once ordered a tubular dropped axle like this, wanting it narrowed 2" overall. They built it by cutting 1" out of each side, making it very difficult to bend the steering arms enough to get a good turning radius. Be sure yours gets narrowed in the middle!

This type of axle also works well on dual leaf front suspensions as found on early GM and Mopar cars, as well as pickups into the 50s. Mounting the axle is very simple with dual leaf springs, where the springs function to carry the car weight as well as control the position of the axle. You can lower the vehicle by dearching the springs or flipping the axle from mounting below the spring to above the spring but problems with

A tubular front axle can certainly be a thing of beauty, though the design lends itself to four-bar suspension rather than split wishbones.

the axle hitting the bottom of the frame often occur. Since the forward frame has to carry the engine weight as well as the suspension stresses, "C"ing the frame for axle clearance usually doesn't work out too well. Merely cutting out the frame for clearance makes the frame too weak and a raised contour to restore strength generally interferes with the sheet metal.

Since many of those cars with parallel leafs springs already have a pretty deeply dropped stock front axle, caution should be exercised with additional drops. As the axle gets deeper, it has more leverage against the leaf springs which provide location and alignment. The very nicely made new dropped axles with CNC machined ends welded to a tube center will have the same leverage problem. Leaf springs with a reduced leaf count, or monoleaf springs may also be more susceptible to this axle torque problem. Heavy braking and steering forces (when steered along the frame rail) can use that leverage to twist the axle on the springs, radically changing the caster.

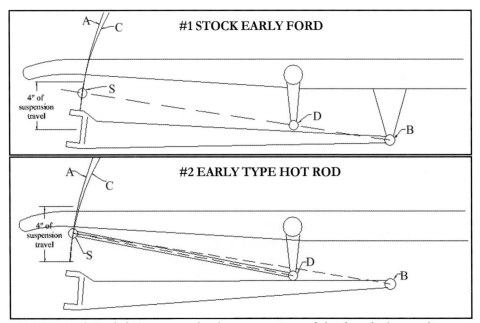

#1, Original Ford design correctly places rear pivot of the drag link on a line between radius rod pivot and the spring eye to spring perch junction. Many say the drag link should be parallel to the radius, but that is only true when a 4 bar is used. #2, Here we see that spring eye to spring perch junction raised due to a spring with a flatter arch or a modified crossmember spring mount. When those techniques are used to lower a car, some bumpsteer is incurred as the rear pivot of the drag link is off line, but since the change is minimal and axle travel is limited we will not notice it to any great extent.

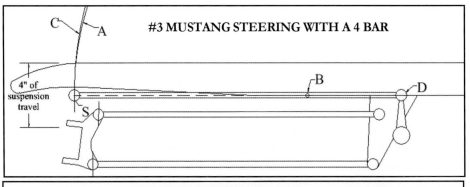

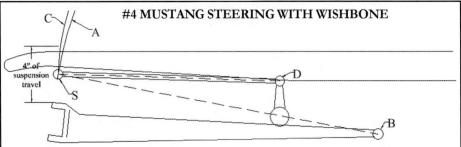

#3, When Mustang side rail drag link steering is used with a 4 bar, the link should be parallel to the bars and as near the same length as possible. #4, With a longer single bar radius rod we revert to wanting the drag link rear pivot on the same line as shown in the first illustration of the stock Ford. Since the drag link pivot is far from the ideal position a car set up this way will exhibit some strong bumpsteer action.

Wheel hop similar to a rear axle under acceleration can even occur. A cross steering design, going to the right side spindle rather than the left front, will be preferred as the twisting force will not occur.

Speaking of steering, the tie rods and drag links from the steering box should be as long and as level as possible to avoid bumpsteer. Bumpsteer was discussed in Chapter Two as a change in toe-in or steering angle as the wheels travel vertically. It is created by uncoordinated suspension versus steering geometry, uncommanded by the driver. Obviously this is something to be avoided in any suspension system.

STEERING BOX ADJUSTMENT

Adjusting vintage steering boxes is a widely misunderstood subject. It seems like every well-meaning mechanic wants to diddle around with the set screw and jam nut readily visible on the box cover plate. Before you take a wrench to the " adjuster" take a look at our suggestions regarding steering boxes in Chapter Four.

STEERING LINKAGE

Most early axle suspension used a steering box that pulls a drag link back and forth along the left front frame rail. The

Illus. page 28&29 - Pete&Jake's

majority of aftermarket power steering conversions for solid axles will follow that pattern. It is important that from a side view, the steering drag link is parallel to, and as close as possible to the same length, as the radius rod. In the case of parallel front leaf springs the imaginary line between the rear spring eye and the axle to spring junction point operate the same as the radius rod mentioned above, in terms of geometry. You will hopefully see that the similar length and angle concept just mentioned is an application of the Arc Length Theory explained in Chapter Two. In essence this solid axle steering design becomes another type of four-bar linkage.

The next diagrams are offered through the courtesy of the fine folks at Pete & Jakes Hot Rod Parts. Although it focuses on the Mustang steering box this presents an excellent illustration of just how a side-steer system works on a solid axle suspension with different arrangements. Both the good and the bad are shown so you can come to understand the difference.

Since a properly located side steering system often leads to a steering column mounted very low, which can interfere with foot pedal access inside the car, cross-steering has become more popular.

The '35-'48 Fords are the earliest example of cross steering that became

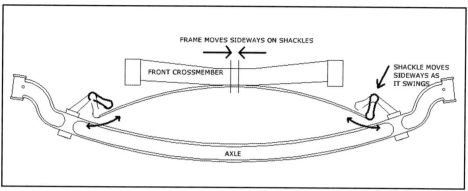

A frame mounted with a tranverse spring moves freely side to side on the shackles. Laterial movement not only occurs from bumps and conering, but is a continuous action resulting from any suspension movement. There are cases where laterial movement is restricted by still working shackles, or shackles that don't swing at all because the spring amin leaf is too short.

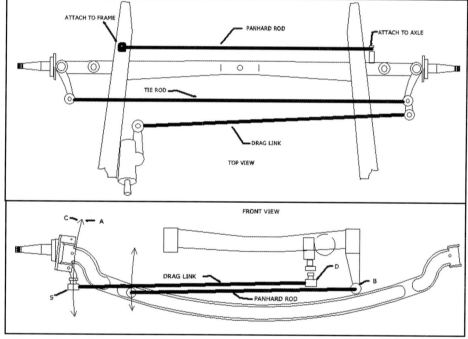

Upper: A panhard rod is used to control lateral movement between frame and axle. It can be mounted in front or behind the axle. Be sure it doesn't interfere with tie rod, which moves closer to the axle when th spindles are turned full right or left. Lower: Lateral control of axle must be relative the drag link for correct geometry during vertical suspension movement. Because the panhard rod pivots at both ends, correct geometry is based on the parallelogram - the drag link and panhard rod should be parallel and as close to the same length as possible. As part of the axle-spindle assm the steering ball on the spindle arm (S) travels in arc (A) equal to the length of the panhard rod, centered at the point (B) parallel to the Panhard rod. Point S also travels an arc (C) centered at the other end of the drag link (D). If drag link and Panhard rod are parallel the arcs will be very close and steering will not be affected.

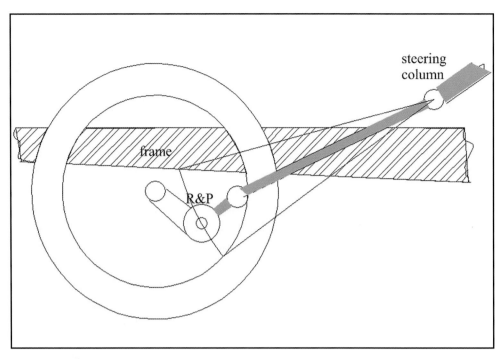

Mounting the rack & pinion to the axle does eliminate bumpsteer since both components move vertically in unison. However, the steering shaft is now on an angle with motion arc which is not vertical. Therefore the effective front to rear length of the shaft changes. Now the steering input shaft requires a connector that allows for that length change yet is secure in rotation, similar to how the car's transmission driveshaft must operate.

Since vehicle weight is being carried on the spindle that weight is pushing up against the axle. Thus the thrust bearing must be on the bottom side to carry that weight. Many rodders forget that the thin shims used to take up any end play in the kingpin joint must be placed on the top side of the joint to avoid being asked to carry weight along with the thrust bearing, which causes damage and hard steering when assembled incorrectly.

common. The advantages are that the column tends to be higher in the car for pedal clearance, but more importantly, bumpsteer is generally less likely to occur than with a side steer as discussed above. The reason is that since the rear pivot of the radius rod with tranverse springs, and the rear eye of parallel leaves are often so far back in the chassis that it's difficult to have a side steer drag link anywhere near the right length needed to minimize bumpsteer. Since the cross-steer mounts to the left hand side of frame just as the cross spring and parallel springs do, getting the draglink nearer the ideal length is much easier to accomplish. Then by having the steering box pitman arm shaped correctly it is fairly easy to have it parallel to the left to right tie rod, thus again minimizing bumpsteer. If you are getting the idea here that to avoid bumpsteer with solid axle steering we need to consider the system as a four-bar, you are very correct! Always think about how the line of action of the suspension relates to the steering linkage and it will become clear how important your understanding of the significance of four-bar geometry really is.

Again, we are favored with superb illustrations from the Pete & Jakes catalog which show how cross-steering should be arranged. You may not be using the Vega box which is explained in the illustrations, but any similar cross steering system will operate in the same essential fashion.

Be cautious when considering a rack and pinion mounted on an axle (see the nearby illustration). If you mount the rack to the frame, the arc of the tie rods will cause bumpsteer. As the axle moves vertically in normal travel, the tie rods move in an arc, pulling the wheels left and right. If you mount the rack to the axle, unsprung weight will increase, which affects ride and handling, but you won't have any bumpsteer. It will, however be absolutely necessary to have a secure, long lasting, lubricated yet sealed sliding joint in the steering connection. In the real world that has been extremely difficult to achieve. As the axle goes up and down, the length of that connection must change. In short, racks on axles have been often tried, with generally poor results.

It is sometimes tempting to consider swapping the spindles side for side, particularly when a rear mounted (suicide style) spring perch is used with a transverse spring to get a very low ride height. The Ackerman principle says that a suspension must develop toe-out in a turn since the inner wheel has to follow a smaller turning circle than the outer. The short version of this principle is that a rear steer spindle will have the outer tie rod end inboard of the spindle, and a front steer outboard. When you reverse the spindle, toe-in occurs in a turn, causing the wheels to skid or exert a side load in that turn. Handling suffers since the tires are skidding, sometimes one and then the other. The steering wheel will jerk when you back up, due to this misaligned wheel tracking. The early T buckets with skinny wire wheels often experienced failed spokes due to this effect. That's why the wheels sold today are wider for more strength to better resist these side loads.

When it comes to straight axles there are plenty of options, this owner opted for a chrome plated, forged axle suspended by a buggy spring with four bars, and tube shocks.

If you have to reverse the spindles, either replace the steering arms with properly aligned ones, or heat and bend (slow cool only - NO WATER) the arms to get the outer tie rod ends outboard of the kingpin for proper Ackerman. You probably can't get it perfect, but some is better than none. Note: Chapter Two includes a series of Ackerman illustrations.

When a dropped axle is installed, it is usually necessary to drop the steering arms as well so that the tie rod doesn't hit the frame, or radius rods. The old way was to heat and bend the steering arms (remember, heat to a nice deep red, bend, then cool them as slowly as possible). SoCal's new axles have a unique end shape that allows greater turning radius with less arm bend-

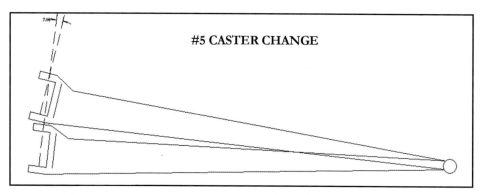

#5 CASTER CHANGE

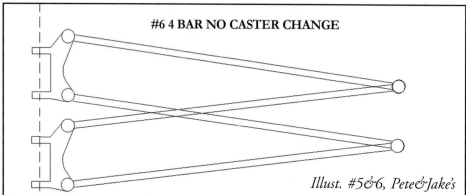

#6 4 BAR NO CASTER CHANGE

Illust. #5&6, Pete&Jake's

#5, Original or long split radius rods will exhibit some caster change as they rotate up and down with suspension travel. Ride quality can be compromised by the binding created between the spring, shackles and crossmember mount.
#6, Note that a four bar linkage acts as a parallelogram and there is no caster change as one or both wheels go over a bump.

This builder used a clever old time trick when using a dropped axle. Notice how the 46-48 Ford style radius rod has a nice rise in it, in the perfect place, making it is easier to pass the tie rod and drag link under the radius rod.

ing required. You can also buy new bolt-on steering arms from a number of sources, in a variety of shapes, or various bend depths.

Continuing the subject of spindles, be sure that the kingpins are properly installed. The bushings must be reamed to size after installation. This can be done with tools sold thru rod shops, or in a real good machine shop. They may have the proper reamer, or can also use a Sunnen piston pin hone machine to do the job even better. Kingpin sets are also available with molded plastic bushings, or needle bearings which have less friction for easier steering, and do not require reaming. The thrust bearing MUST be installed to carry vehicle weight, and therefore goes between the bottom of the axle and the spindle. If your steering effort is real heavy, check here first.

You hear a lot of conversation about the different types of radius rods that are used on straight-axle suspensions, with different types of axle construction. Nostalgic hot rods have made a huge comeback in the last few years, bringing this question up to a new generation of hot rodders. I love seeing the interest and respect the younger guys have for traditional cars, but it seems that the same learning curve we went through earlier is being experienced again as well. Maybe some tech info on this question will help prevent experiencing the more difficult parts of repeating history.

What are the best combinations of split wishbone, hairpin, and four-bar radius rod systems versus the forged or cast I-beams and round tube axles?

The issue at heart is how the axle's flexibility, or the lack of that property, affects the action of the radius rods. If the axle and radius rod types are both very stiff, those parts can be overstressed, and failures may occur. Welds, brackets and bolts may fail, causing a very dangerous situation. If those parts are sufficiently strong (or

improved to that level) so no failures will occur, [but] very stiff handling and ride quality will be the result.

This difficulty is caused by the need for each wheel to react to, and only to, the bump it sees on its side of the road. If it cannot react because the suspension has been built very stiff and heavily enough to not fail, the car will have to hop over that bump rather than riding over it. That will quite obviously cause the poor ride quality and poor handling spoken of above. This need for an acceptable level of flexibility is really the reason IFS (Independent Front Suspension) was developed, yet many cars just look better with an axle. So how do we get the proper combination of flexibility and strength?

Historically speaking, forged steel axles with an I-beam section were the first to be made. A

Track style cowl steering and friction shocks lend an Old School look to this suspension, while the traditional hairpin radius rods are modernized with a street rod urethane bushed rod end used as the frame mount connection. Combining the old style with some modern tech can work very well after serious thought goes into the design.

very good grade of steel was used, combining strength with durability. I have a DVD of the 1940 World's Fair, showing an original 1940 Ford I-beam axle being twisted three complete times around! This obviously took a good bit of force to accomplish, but the point for us to see is that the axle does actually have the ability to twist. Ford's wishbone design did not require the axle to twist when the suspension moved. Since both the axle and the wishbone were mounted to the frame at its center, the axle and wishbone assembly had the ability to rotate in order to ride over bumps

Controlling the axle is a bit more complicated with transverse springs, also known as buggy springs. A wishbone, like Ford originally used, is actually ideal, and provided excellent positioning with incomparable flexibility. Unfortunately, it often interferes with the installation of late model V-8 engines. Split wishbones were developed to solve that problem, but they created a new difficulty. Since one wheel cannot rise without twisting the axle, roll rates are very high. That creates pretty good cornering on a smooth road, but

rough ride and poor traction on bumps. Forged axles are much preferred with split wishbones since their inherent flexibility and toughness allows them to accept this twisting force. The axle actually becomes a giant sway bar. The twisting forces can lead to failures of rod ends, clevis bolts, and even axles made with methods other than forging. As mentioned earlier, fabricated axles in particular used to see a lot of problems with T buckets in the old days, and will do the same today.As the early dirt track racers sought higher speeds and better handling, they found that the quite stiff roll resistance of the split wishbone radius rod set up was working against them. To get a more freely articulating suspension, the hairpin radius rod came into use. Note that one style is called the Kurtis style, named for the very successful builder of Midget, Sprint, and Indy cars from the 30s and 40s. The hairpin itself has the ability to flex in torsion, thus freeing up the assembly and not requiring the axle to twist.

Then the lightweight '37-'40' Ford tube axle from the V8-60 cars began to show up. It not only looked good, but reduced unsprung weight and helped handling. Since it would not twist like the forged I-beams, the more flexible hairpin radius rods became more important. I cannot prove it, but I think that this very stiffness of the early Ford tube axles led directly to the use of the four-bar system. Since fabricated round tube axles have the same attributes and problems as the early 60 Horse Ford axles, the same logic applies to them as well.

A four-bar system is probably the ultimate in controlling the axle's posi-

When it comes to controlling the position of the straight axle in a variety of driving situations, the 4 bar does an admirable job. It looks good, exhibits no caster change, and no binding during up and down motion.

tion in the chassis while allowing free motion. Since the axle doesn't need to twist at all, the axle caster doesn't change with travel, as it does with split bones and hairpins. It's also very handy to have such an easy way to adjust caster, also an advantage of hairpins made with adjustable clevis ends at the axle. Since the four-bar does not attempt to twist the axle at all, the stress on the four-bar itself is reduced. Very good handling with quite acceptable ride quality often results. Broken links, mounts and damaged axles are a rarity with a four-bar system for the same reason.

I-beam axles are available in both cast and forged versions. As you can imagine from the earlier discussions, the forged axle is better able to resist stress. The cast axle will be much more rigid, which actually works against suspension

function unless a four bar is used to remove twisting stress from the axle. We are also seeing aluminum axles, which should prove to work quite well, given the properties of the alloy being used. I would expect them to act the same as a forged axle in use. Drilling the axle, unless taken to an extreme, shouldn't have much affect on the axle. If anything, the forged axle will become a bit less stiff, as well as being lighter and cool looking. But be warned, drilling a forged axle will take more time and better tools than you probably expect! Drilling wishbones shouldn't be a problem as long as good judgment is being used in terms of hole size. I'm going to make the dangerous assumption that no one who is smart enough to read will be dumb enough to drill a wishbone without welding tube sleeves back into

The layout of the drag link and radius rod on this ultra clean machine look a lot like the diagrams on the upper part of page 28. In other, this is a system that will likely work very well, and exhibit little or no bumpsteer.

This suicide perch design gets the car low without the use of a dropped axle, but the reversed early Ford spindles exhibit reversed Ackerman. Understeer and tire scrub in a turn will be the result. Bending the steering arms outboard and using a longer tie rod will make a big improvement.

the holes! Otherwise,, those WILL fail in short order!

In my opinion, the flexible forged I-beam axle with a four-bar is the best riding, handling, and safest combination. That forged I-beam will also work well with hairpins or split bones, but the added stiffness will detract from ride and handling. A less flexible cast I-beam or tube axle will certainly do well with the four bar, and less so with the hairpins. Split bones with the more rigid axles will be the worst case, and need sufficiently strong bolts and brackets to prevent failures, while likely riding hard and handling pretty stiffly. A historically correct hot rod, or personal taste, may point you to a less than ideal combination, just be sure to take the added stresses into account in your fabrication work.

An excellent set of drawings and another explanation of these concepts can be found in the Pete and Jakes catalog. Jerry and Jason Slover were kind enough to allow a portion of those drawings to be included in the next illustration (some of which we've recreated). You'll find some very good info regarding many aspects of axle suspension explained and illustrated very well.

A tube axle with buggy spring and 4 bars - note the pockets at the end of each leaf for a plastic button to minimize friction.

36

BUGGY SPRINGS

One of the simplest, yet critical aspects of a buggy spring install is the spring itself. Friction between the leaves is the culprit, as that must be overcome before the axle can move in response to road bumps. Posie pioneered the use of plastic buttons in the spring leafs to improve the spring. You can also purchase urethane strips molded with a lip to keep them in place over the spring. We often use them as an improvement in rear springs too. According to Mike at Eaton Spring, square cut spring ends are the cheapest to make and the hardest to get moving. Diamond cutting is better, and rounding the ends and tapering the leaf thickness aids even more in improving spring flexibility. You can, and should, detail your springs this way, or buy them already done. The idea is to ease the transition from one leaf to the next in search of a reduction in that initial "un-sticking"of the leaf stack. Original Ford springs were in fact rounded and tapered, with a grease groove fed by a hollow center bolt and a grease fitting. Henry really did know what he was doing!

Eaton Spring Company uses an electrical induction furnace to soften the leaf spring steel enough to allow tapering the thickness of the ends. The flared spring ends are also being trimmed to a rounded shape.

The induction furnace at Eaton Spring is also used to stamp a dimple into the leaf which serves to retain the plastic slide button used to minimize interleaf friction.

This set up uses '45-'54 Chevy spindles and exhibits correct Ackerman properties with the front steer tie rod ends outboard of the kingpin. This one will drive right without any odd handling.

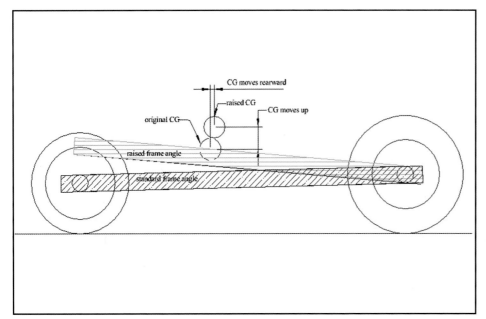

CG moves rearward

raised CG

original CG — CG moves up

raised frame angle

standard frame angle

The frame rotates around the rear wheel center as the nose is raised. That rotation has the effect of moving the CG up and back, but since the rear movement is much smaller than the rise, you will lose more in handling than you gain in traction.

Proper alignment of the spring perches, shackles and springs is also critical. If the spring is twisted relative to the perches, the edges of the leaves experience friction that we don't want. Swivel perches are available to help with this, as well as Posie's new swivel shackles. Their catalog and website have excellent illustrations if this point needs clarification. Be sure the spring length is correct so that the shackles are at a 45 degree angle and do not bottom out in the perches.

Many people really struggle with installing the spring into the shackles. The original spring eye went down, so a tool was used to spread the spring enough to flatten the arch as when loaded, so that the shackles would reach. Our springs commonly have reversed eyes for extra lowering, but the eye going up cannot accept the stretching tool. If the car is fully assembled with all the weight in place, you can support the ends of the spring on a short piece of 2X4. The spring will slide outward along the board until the shackles reach. If the car is incomplete, it is easiest to disassemble the spring and mount the easily flexed main leaf alone into the shackles. The other leafs are then added, aligned by a long center bolt and clamped in place to compress them until the spring is reassembled. Those swivel perches also

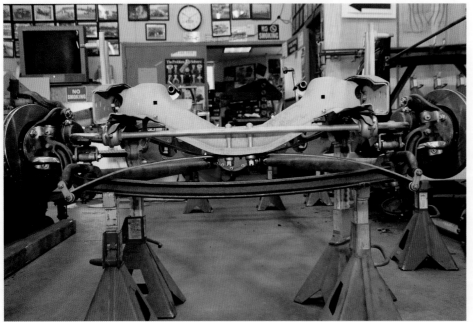

The 1940 Ford axle set up here has just the main leaf installed. This allows an approximation of the finished fully loaded ride height, and eliminates the huge struggle that spreading a complete multi-leaf spring to assemble the shackles can present.

help since you can loosen the nut enough to "stretch" the shackle to the spring. Don't fight the spring - think about these tips and eliminate the frustration.

Monoleaf and fiberglass springs are one more attempt to reduce interleaf friction 'cuz there isn't any. They do lack the convenience of being able to be tuned by adding or subtracting leafs, but work great if you nail the required rate. Coil-overs do even better if you have the space, the style of build, and the ability to properly mount them. They are probably the very best ride, but their high tech look can get a little out of place with some build styles. Linkages can be built to hide them, but the increased friction loss in all the pivot points lose much of their advantages, and often caused mixed reviews in practicality.

Setting the alignment on a solid axle is simple, and can be performed in your home shop with simple tools such as a digital level and a tape measure. Look for around 5-6 degrees positive caster and 1/8" toe-in as a good starting point.

SPECIAL STYLES

This is a good point in our discussion to look at a couple of special types of solid axle suspension. The first is the Gasser look, with a pronounced rake toward a very high nose of the car. It's a look popular with vintage enthusiasts, but it has many downsides. The first is that today's drag racers have come to realize that the idea of raising the nose to get more rear tire traction simply was wrong. The entire idea may have come from a common exercise done in Engineering schools and drag racing tech articles

which are used to determine the vertical as well as fore/aft position of a car's CG (center of gravity). The car is weighed front and rear then raised in front a certain distance and reweighed. Through a series of calculations involving Algebra and Trigonometry the change in front to rear weight bias is used to calculate the position of the CG. It really doesn't change the position of the CG. more than a few inches, but it was one of the ideas tried in an attempt to go quicker before better chassis and tires came along.

Although raising the nose does move the CG up and rearward, a quick study of the physics involved will make it clear that traction is more easily improved with traction arm devices, proper springs and shocks, and better tires. The downsides of a high nose are more body roll and high-speed instability due to that raised CG. As speeds continued to rise the extra aerodynamic drag also conspired to erase any real traction advantages that might have been gained. That's the reason serious drag racers have abandoned this concept. The disadvantages for a street driven car should be obvious. Very few modern hot

Straight axles come in a variety of flavors. This builder chose a chrome, forged I-beam axle, supported by 4 bars, with cross-steer.

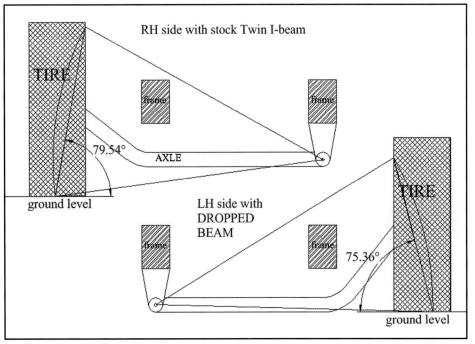

As the dropped beams lower the truck, they also put the tire higher in the rotation of the axle from it's frame pivot. That causes exaggerated camber change with even worse handling and tire wear than the stock height factory arrangement.

rod or race car fabrication companies build this type suspension for those reasons.

But like so many choices we make when building our hot rods. Logic may be trumped by the desire to replicate a certain nostalgic style. You just need to be honest with yourself as to whether the style outweighs function and safety.

Another interesting variation involves converting a solid axle into a special type of IFS. The Allard race cars and some British club racers in the 40s and 50s used an axle split and pivoted in the center to get many of the advantages of an IFS in an axle world. They did not also split the tie rod to match and therefore had a lot of bumpsteer. The tie rod must be split with the inner pivots matching the axle pivot points. Then camber is adjusted by controlling the heights of the axle inner pivots as well as the spring height, so coil-overs are a natural for this application. Several companies used to offer axle kits with this design but the simple fact that they never sold well caused them to be discontinued. If you are a clever fabricator that under stands the split axle

AND steering concept, you can build your own version that will surprise you in how well they ride and handle while preserving the axle look we like.

A variation on the split axle concept was used by Ford on their pickups from '65-'89. Dubbed the "Twin I-beam" was an attempt to make a better driving front suspension than a plain solid axle while avoiding the perceived complexity and possibly less robust nature of true IFS such as used by GM from 1960 on. Camber change was minimized by having each axle swing from the opposite side of the frame rail. However, that made coordinating the steering difficult as the tie rods would have to cross over one another. Since the designers had to compromise on the steering geometry, these trucks became known for accelerated tire wear and strange handling when pushed hard.

Those difficulties become even worse with wider tires and dropped version of the axles. Naturally, as a wider tire is used, any camber change as is inherent is the Twin I-beam system will tip the wheel enough so that very rapid wear occurs on the edges of the tire. That same camber change creates problems with a dropped beam axle. Since the dropped axle raises the wheel higher in the camber change curve, the already heavy camber change is exaggerated even more. Add a wider tire in that mix and you have a real strange handling, tire-destroying mess. That is probably why manufacturers of dropped beams come and go while true IFS systems remain on the market.

One of the best ways to assemble the necessary components for a successful axle installation is to review the ads, websites, and catalogs. Then find a dealer who really understands the set up and follow his advice. Maybe even buy the parts from the man who knows the facts rather than just has the cheapest prices. Good advice is worth the price! Much of this knowledge is considered common amongst the graybeards, but are new to the younger guys. Check around, ask around, and spend the time to tune your axle setup.

After considering all the advantages and difficulties of a solid axle suspension, you may actually decide that an IFS will be better suited to the mission of your hot rod project. The generally better ride and handling may be more desirable after all. By choosing right design and level of style, an IFS can look very good indeed under either open or closed fender cars. A very large number of suppliers offer kits for IFS swaps while the more clever rodders may in some cases choose to adapt an OEM design or even design and fabricate their own IFS. The place many rodders go wrong is when the arrangement of control arms and steering are altered to fit under a fender or to change the track width. Track width mismatches are all too often the cause of an unsuccessful suspension swap. Be very leery of any design that requires special length control arms or tie rod ends. Modifications can be done successfully when the geometry has been studied and understood but many designs have major flaws in that department. The next chapter will discuss how IFS functions and should prove helpful in deciding which route is the best for your car!

The reversed Early Ford spindle used here exhibit reversed Ackerman. Although the modern wider Hallcraft wire wheels will resist that sideways push better than the old skinny ones, the wheels are allowing enough room for this rodder to bend the steering arms outward to correct the Ackerman. That will be hard on the chrome but easier on the driver's nerves when driving the car!

Chapter Four

Independent Front Suspension

Sophisticated Suspension for Hot Rods Old and New

By and large, IFS (Independent Front Suspension) is an integral feature of most contemporary hot rods. There will always be the nostalgic themed early hot rods, which will generally use some type of the solid axle suspension just discussed in the last chapter. For the rodder that wants to really drive his car with all the advantages of modern cars; better handling, improved ride, less driver fatigue on long trips, and overall safety, the IFS will nearly always be the preferred suspension. The advice often given is that if you expect to never drive more than 55

If you're willing to give up the nostalgic look, there are a variety of IFS options available from a wide range of manufacturers. Be sure you buy from a well known company, a company that can explain the advantages of using one of their suspension kits.

MPH and less than 100 miles from home, you may be reasonably happy with vintage tires, steering brakes and suspension. If on the other hand a 500 mile weekend is more your style, you are going to want an IFS on your hot rod.

IFS systems were developed as a way to disconnect the action of one wheel from its partner on the other side of the car. By doing so a bump affecting one wheel should have no effect on the other. (Later we'll discuss anti-sway bars as a way to control weight transfer but also has the effect of re-connecting the wheels at some level). Since each wheel now has less unsprung weight (weight that has to be moved to allow the wheel to react to a bump) with fewer heavy suspension components attached, that wheel can better follow road surface variations. Improved traction is achieved since a wheel off the road cannot help the car turn, stop, or accelerate. Further, with the wheel now able to react to the bump without disturbing the rest of the chassis ride quality will improve as well.

Don't let anyone ever tell you that a good handling car has to ride like a dump truck. It's a matter of having the right springs, shocks, tires and general suspension layout. Then it all has to be tuned for proper balance.

Historically, attempts to design an IFS began as early as cars themselves were being built. There was actually an early version called the De Dion type, after the French manufacturer who first used it in the 1910s. It was also used on a few early Indy cars, front wheel drive Cords, and Maseratis

The first really practical IFS systems were evolved from solid axle technology and used the kingpins that were so familiar...

...with basically similar upper and lower trunnion pins on the control arm ends, to serve the same dual steer and spindle control functions accomplished by ball joints in the modern era.

A cleanly installed IFS can work fine on a fenderless car, even though it is a bit more complex than a straight axle. What you gain is far better roadability for a real travelling hot rod.

in the Fifties. It actually combines a solid axle to control the wheels with half shafts to transfer power from the transaxle to the wheels. Being unnecessarily heavy and complex, it fell out of favor.

In the early 1930s common production cars led by the 1934 Plymouth/Dodge began to use an IFS type that included a kingpin. It tuned out the MOPAR design actually infringed on patents that GM held but wouldn't themselves begin to use until later in the 1930s, so MOPAR went back to solid axles until 1939. GM converted to different forms of IFS for most of their cars by 1934, while Ford never went to IFS until 1949. Since ball joints as we know them today had not yet become practical, an arrangement similar to a solid axle was used. A separate spindle swiveling on a kingpin which was mounted to a vertical part (often called a knuckle or upright) similar to the end of an axle was used. Outer pins and bushing called trunnions were the used at the outer ends of the control arms, connected to the upper and lower ends of the upright. This three piece assembly serves the same purpose as the spindle and ball joints on a more modern IFS.

This combination of trunnion pins and kingpin allowed the same range of motion for steering and suspension as the more modern ball joints we all know today. It is very rugged but is relatively heavy which creates a negative effect on ride and handling. Another disadvantage is that as the caster is adjusted the trunnions pins tend to get out of square with

The Delphi style power steering box is an exciting development in the upgrading of vintage IFS systems, and can be manufactured in reverse rotation form for specialty applications such as the '49-'51 Ford shown here.

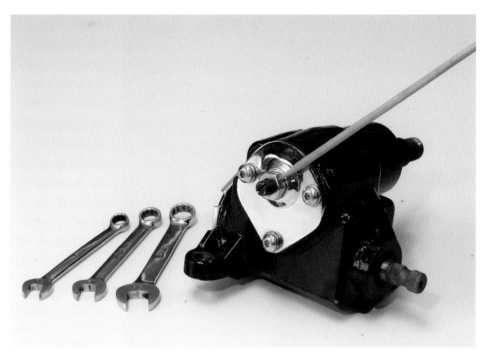

It seems like everyone thinks this screw and jam nut adjusts the steering box, but all it does is adjust the end play of the sector shaft leading to the pitman arm. That sector shaft end play adjustment must be done first, but THEN the gear mesh adjusted....

steering arm and height of the outer tie rod end. That would spell problems with both turning radius and bumpsteer, as has been seen on such swaps that are on the market. In the opinion of this writer it is generally better to rebuild and upgrade the original suspension with disc brakes than to alter it with new and originally unrelated parts. Dropped spindles, better shock absorbers, steering box and linkage kits are also available to upgrade the suspension that came in the car.

Alignment can be more difficult than a modern ball joint suspension. Adjustment tech-

their bushing and create wear. The simple fact that there are more connections than a ball joint system tends to add up to more total play in the system. That makes maintenance more important.

There are cases where this early kingpin style IFS has been converted to more modern ball joints replacing the trunnion pins, also involving a swap to a later spindle that already mounts disc brakes. This concept is interesting and certainly has advantages in terms of maintenance and parts availability, but there are a number of common pitfalls that can make the change easier to discuss than to pull off successfully. The position of the inner and outer control arms pivots are particularly critical in maintaining the integrity of a suspension's geometry. If the swap to ball joints includes a change in the position of those pivot points, bumpsteer will likely be introduced. Also, the swapped spindle may also have a different length to the

To adjust gear mesh the cover nuts and bolts must be very slightly loosened. Then one will be an eccentric bolt which will be rotated to alter the gear mesh before retightening the cover fasteners.

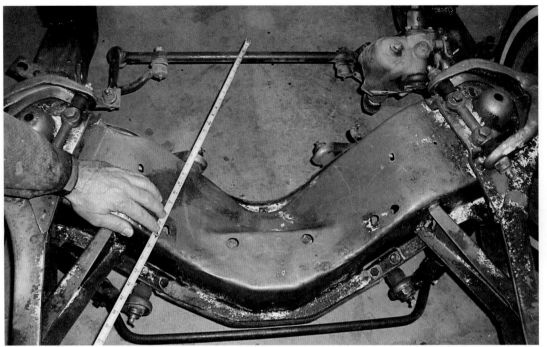

Seen again on a 49-51 Ford IFS, the inner tie rods need to be in line with the LCA hinge pivot axis, whether you are converting to a R&P or a conventional steering gear. Ford learned this lesson and relocated their inner tie rod ends as the basic IFS design continued into the '52-'53 cars.

niques are not all that difficult but will be a complete mystery to most modern mechanics. The '39-'54 GM cars have a camber adjustment that is accessed through a hole in the upper trunnion bushing normally occupied by the grease fitting! It is essential to find an original shop manual that goes into the exact methods used. Camber and toe-in are not really a problem, but caster is a common problem. One of the major pitfalls of retaining your original IFS on hot rod is that they were generally designed to be easier to steer by using very little positive caster, or even negative caster. That setting minimizes steering effort as there is little tendency to raise the car's weight as the wheels steer, but it also translates to poor high speed stability, which can be enhanced by higher positive caster settings. Adding power steering increases this problem.

It is difficult to add more positive caster since the range of adjustment is quite limited, but there is a way to cheat the upper control arm rearward to shift the range of caster adjustment more into the positive range. If the upper control arm does not incorporate the shock absorber, as is done with most GM cars but rather simply is bolted to the frame, the control arm shaft can be moved forward in the bushings.

To do this support the car weight at the lower control arm and unbolt the upper arm shaft from the frame. Then rotate the shaft forward within the bushings, which will then move the actual upper arm rearward on the chassis when the shaft is re-bolted to the frame. Plan on every 3/16" movement amounting to 1 degree of additional positive caster.

Steering varied from really good to really awful in terms of bumpsteer. The best generally have the inner tie rod end pivots in line with the lower control arm inner pivot hinge line. With the lower arm hinge axis forming a V with the point toward the rear of the car, as with the Packard, Buick, Cadillac, Olds and Pontiacs, a central idler arm with three holes to mount the pitman arm and inner tie rod ends in a roughly triangular pattern. Their lower cost brother Chevrolets from 1939-48 had to suffer along with a really poor system with parallel lower control arm hinge axis that connected a proper length LH tie rod to the steering box pitman arm and an overly long RH tie rod, thus creating RH side bumpsteer. The later '49-'54 Chevy changed to the V type lower arm arrangement and the central idler just described. Since the '53-'62 Corvette used the same basic IFS with the entire steering assembly moved down to allow a lower engine position, the same description applies. The '39-up MOPARS also used the V type design and generally had pretty good geometry.

Ford seems to have misunderstood the geometry in their for IFS for '49-'51 Ford and Mercury, as evidenced by the fact that they changed the steering geometry for the better when they continued the '49-'51 design thru '52-'53. The issue was the location of the inner tie rod end pivots which were too far apart in the first version but later relocated to the V type linkage as described above.

Loose steering boxes are common among these cars. The '49-'51 Fords have a very unusual steering box that not only is reverse rotation compared to most cars, but also has the sector and worm shafts at a 45 degree angle to one another rather than the more common 90 degree relationship. It is believed that the strange angle builds in more play than other designs, as evidenced by 8000 original mile '50 Ford museum cars with the same ½ turn of slop as seen on high mileage cars. Just as with the tie rod redesign, the '52-'53 cars have a more usual steering box layout. No amount of rebuilding or adjustment seems to help.

As mentioned earlier, almost everyone tries to adjust vintage steering boxes by fiddling with the jam nut and screw that is obvious on the top of the box at the end of the sector shaft. All that does is to take up end play in the sector shaft while having no effect whatsoever on gear mesh. The worm gear end-play is typically adjusted at the top end where the main steering shaft coming down the column mast jacket enters the box body. End-play there is adjusted by adding or subtracting shims. The box cover that has the sector shaft jam nut and screw generally has a way to adjust gear mesh through an eccentric bolt or bushing. Again, your best aid will be an original factory shop manual or Motor Manual both of which can be found as originals or reprints common in the auto literature market.

It is possible to swap a later GM Saginaw type steering box ('70-'81 Camaro for example) into many of these cars. The key point is to first

The true knee action GM IFS systems were this very heavy yet fast wearing a sloppy driving version, shown here on a 1938 Chevy. There isn't much point in trying to adapt this to modern use.

The Second GM IFS was a much better system in that it incorporated A arms just as on modern cars. A lever shock was used as the UCA, and actually worked well, although prone to early wear and relatively low power wheel control.

verify the direction of rotation on the original box and be sure your replacement unit matches. You will find that to be a match on most of the larger GM and MOPAR cars thru the '35-'60 era. There are almost no commercial kits available, but after verifying the rotation it will be a matter of mounting the new box in a way that will allow connection to your steering column and steering linkage. Then a hybrid steering linkage is made using parts that match the new box to the original linkage. This is not a simple job but it is doable.

For the '49-'51 Ford and '49-'54 Chevy, their reverse rotation steering boxes create a problem. As of 2016, the Borgeson and Fatman Fabrication companies have teamed to develop a special new box that does have the correct rotation. Kits for the Fords are now available, while the Chevy kits are under development. The Chevy cars from '55-'70 can use a modified later GM box often identified as the Delphi type. It is similar to the '70s GM Saginaw box, but has an input shaft mounted sensor system similar to that used on power rack and pinion steering. These have proven to be very successful swaps.

Be very careful about swapping in a rack-and-pinion steering system in these cars. The height, and left-to-right distance of the inner tie rod is extremely critical in avoiding bumpsteer. As a general rule these cars actually had decent geometry with the exception of the '39-'48 Chevy noted above. Therefore you will do well to choose and position your rack and pinion so that the inner tie rod on the rack mimics the original inner tie rod position. Then the outer tie rod end being unchanged in terms of position, your steering will work the same as it did originally. Forget all about the old racer's tale that the tie rods must be level. When we discuss bumpsteer geometry in the next drawing you will see that correct tie rod angle is dependent on how it coordinates with the control arms. Being level may occur, but it would be purely coincidental. Unfortunately a great many of the rack-and-pinion conversion kits on the market do not do a great job of following good practice in terms of geometry. Hopefully you will learn enough in this book to discern the difference between the different designs and make the best choice, or be able to design your own.

SHOCKS

The Fords and MOPARS of this era used a modern appearing tube shock that will be very familiar, yet much is to be gained by upgrading them. You can research this by looking at a Monroe shock catalog, finding your part number then looking in the cross index in the back to find the interchanges. You can also find the length and end types of your shock to find modern replacements. As an example in the '49-'56 Ford and '49-'54 Chevy, '49-'57 Pontiac, and '50-'53 Cadillac front suspension, modern high-end shocks listed for a '53-'62 Corvette are a direct interchange. The MOPARS have a really weird mounting for the front shocks. The lower end mounts as usual to the lower control arm but the upper mounts to the UPPER control arm rather than the frame! Since that creates very little length change in the shock it has negligible effect on the suspension. The last few years of the kingpin IFS design changed to a modern mounting inside the coil spring, but earlier cars will vastly benefit from having the upper end mount changed to the frame rail location as shown next.GM began using IFS as early as 1934 with the Chevy Master and Pontiac which using a design referred to as "Knee Action." Later GM cars went to a design with the upper control arm also serving as a lever shock. That design is often unfairly and incorrectly referred to as "Knee Action" which was indeed a truly poor design. Rather, there is nothing inherently wrong with the upper control arm/lever shock method. Many hot rods

There's just not much reason to try to live with erratic vintage drum brakes when easy to install disc kits such as this ECI MOPAR version are just a phone call away. Your safety and comfort are worth the effort!

have successfully retained this design, but supplementing the admittedly weak stock lever shock with a modern tube shock. Refer back to the MOPAR shock mount system shown earlier, and use a '73-'87 Chevy Pickup shock to build a very good performing system.

BRAKES

It's pretty easy for us today to criticize the negative features of these early IFS designs, but the very nature of engineering evolution makes it clear that all responsible designers learn and improve their products as time passes. It is also true that the demands of gravel roads, 45 MPH average speeds and skinny bias ply tires are completely different from what we expect today. There are several suppliers of disc brake kits for these cars, kits which bolt directly to your original spindle.

Don't forget that your original master cylinder must be replaced or at least altered. The issue is that drum brakes require a minimum of 10 psi residual pressure in the lines to prevent the shoes from retracting too far due to the very strong return springs used on drum brakes. Disc brakes cannot tolerate that pressure since they have no return springs and will therefore drag on the rotors and overheat. That need for different valving is the REAL reason the dual master cylinder was developed. Modern cylinders with unequal size reservoirs are typically used with front disc/rear drum applications, the smaller reservoir serving the smaller bore rear wheel cylinders. Equal size reservoir master cylinders are typically used on 4 wheel disc systems and should have the port nearest the cylinder-mounting flange plumbed to the rear brakes. Rear drum brakes can be accommodated with this type master cylinder, by adding an external in-line 10 psi residual pressure valve to the rear drums and a 2 psi residual pressure valve to the front discs.

Best practice will always be to set up your brake system with a modern dual master cylinder. Many kits exist to add to or replace your original master cylinder with a modern dual type. If you just cannot make the master cylinder upgrade due to space or mounting constraints the original single reservoir type can be adapted for disc brakes. Inside the master cylinder you will see a long reaction spring with the outlet end having a stamped metal seat that looks like a hat. It will have 6-8 holes with thin black rubber showing in those holes. This is the original residual pressure valve, which can be disabled by punching thru those holes to allow free flow of brake fluid in and

Rear wheel brakes will always be plumbed to the smaller reservoir when a dual chamber master cylinder is used. If both reservoirs are of equal size the rear is plumbed to the port nearest the pushrod, as shown here.

out of the master cylinder. Then add external in line residual pressure valves as just discussed and you'll be ready to go.

Back to Suspension

We have discussed the Kingpin IFS in detail, but it is important to consider replacing it entirely with ball joint based systems that offer easier service, better parts availability and improved handling along with the lower ride stance that defines most modern hot rods.

Some cars in this era, such as the '39-'54 Chevy, have an IFS that can be unbolted, then a Mustang II based IFS can be easily installed. Some of those kits bolt in while others weld in according to the thoughts of the manufacturer on which is best. For nearly all the rest of the cars in this group, an IFS swap is more complicated. Since the original frames were built with coil spring pockets integrated into the frame rails, a straight-forward crossmember cannot be simply welded in place. The old way to install a modern IFS was labor intensive. The offending coil spring pockets had to be cut off the outside of the frame rail and exterior boxing plates added to fill that void space. Thus the outer frame rail was straightened and allow the installation of a new IFS crossmember. Another way involves cutting off the old front rails and adding new pair built with rectangular tubing, creating straight rails that do accept a new IFS.

Some rodders have the capability to design and fabricate their own front rails. To assist others who lack that capability several companies have developed new front frame stubs. Some of these will be universal in nature and require the installer to fabricate new bumper, radiator and sheet metal mounting points as well as smoothly joining the old and new frame rails. Others are application specific and tended to, especially the radiator core support position, which typically controls the fit of the entire front sheet metal clip.

During the 1950s all the manufacturers, with the exception of Studebaker, (who persisted with the Kingpin IFS until they went out of business) switched to IFS designs based on the newly developed ball joint. The ball joint can swivel in rotation and also change angle as the control arm moves up and down, allowing designers to greatly simplify their IFS by eliminating the trunnion and king pins. There was apparently some concern as to whether the LBJ (lower ball joint) could safely carry the weight of the car, as all the GM cars other than Oldsmobile had the lower stud pointing down so the weight was carried into the ball joint shell rather than pulling out as is modern practice.

The "derby hat" shaped part at left from a single reservoir master cylinder is the residual pressure valve, which can be used is a disc brake application by puncturing the black rubber diagram visible through the holes. Then exterior in line RPV units can be installed which are appropriate for disc or drum brake use.

Olds had it arranged as we do today, and since all the cars evolved into the pin-pointing-up style we use today, it would appear that the concern over ball joint safety was unnecessary.

The very popular MII IFS (based loosely on the '74-'78 Mustang II) is often supplied with tubular control arms, which use ball joints originally designed for a MOPAR UCA (Upper Control Arm). A similar well intended caution as just discussed with the early GM inverted LBJ is occasionally raised as to whether using a ball joint intended for use on an UCA is appropriate for use on a LCA (Lower Control Arm). This practice began since the ball joint in question installs with a screw in thread design that makes the tubular control arms easier to build and cleaner in appearance. The concept first found favor in the NASCAR racing series going back into the early 1960's. Further, and following examination of the actual construction of upper and lower ball joints, shows that there is really no difference in how the upper and lower ball joints are manufactured or how the stud is retained.

First hand examination of a rare failed LBJ revealed that it was never lubricated after installation (probably because we've all gotten used to modern cars which lack any means, or requirement, to be greased). In addition, in this case the castle nut was not properly installed. A LBJ

The nicely sorted out Mustang II IFS is installed on a new 1939 Chevy chassis. The solid bar is used to support the car at its correct ride height during the mockup stage, prior to the vehicle being loaded at its finished weight load.

Wm. Longyard

that failed for lack of proper lubrication and usage can hardly be blamed on the part itself.. Considering that group of facts, the successful experience of hundreds of racers and thousands of hot rodders - all of whom used the same ball joint top and bottom, it appears that there is no real issue with the MII systems with their MOPAR-sourced ball joints.

Modern IFS systems vary widely from good to bad in terms of their design geometry. Some of the most popular of the muscle cars, the '65-'73 Mustang, '64-'72 Chevelle and '67-'69 Camaro are among the worst in that regard. The proof is that an entire industry has arisen to eliminate the flaws and bring those IFS systems up to modern standards. It is important to remember that these designs originated in the late Fifties to early Sixties when speeds and traffic laid fewer demands on cars of this era. Also, when all you had was a skinny Nylon bias ply tire with 4"-6" of actual tread, things like bumpsteer simply weren't a concern. Add today's power, speed, braking, traffic density and so on, and the need is apparent - these favorite classics should handle and ride on par with modern family cars. Modified properly, these vintage IFS designs have proven capable of run-

ning side by side with any modern muscle cars. So let's analyze what is going on in terms of design and equipment to make that transformation possible.

We took a look at Arc Length Theory in the second chapter, and now understand that different length control arms (whether they are used for the hood hinge or suspension) have a change in effective length as they rotate. In a later chapter we will discuss how a rear suspension uses the very same theory and level control arms to keep the axle square in the chassis during body roll. Now we'll take the next step and see how manipulating the length and angle of control arms in a front suspension can be used to improve handling.

The basic issue is maintaining a maximum contact patch where the rubber hits the road. Since the only traction available is the area

Lots to see here....a mounted front anti-away bar with good clearances, good ball joint to spindle angles, a coil-over replacement set up bar, and large OEM type disc brakes. Since additional positive caster is used with a power rack and pinion, special taller anti bumpsteer outer tie rod ends are used to compensate for the spindle being rotated back and the front-steer tie rod position being raised.

Wm. Longyard

This '59-'64 Pontiac spindle exhibits the inverted lower ball joint design, initially used until more confidence was gained in the ability for more normally mounted ball joints to carry the weight of the car.

where each tire tread contacts pavement, it logically follows that best handling will result when that grip is maintained. Any skidding resulting from improper Ackerman, non-zero scrub radius, weather, too small a tire, or bad camber control will bring us closer to a loss of control. Modern sticky and wider tires help adhesion, but only when the geometry is right. In fact, the greater traction of modern tires will detract from handling characteristics when poor geometry results in bumpsteer or bad camber action, causing the car to react unpredictably.

Many '60s musclecars have flaws in the design of their suspensions. Those flaws were hidden by the limited traction of the hard, skinny tires of their design era with limited traction. The greater traction of newer fatter tires will actually highlight those design deficiencies.

A quick history will illustrate this point. Referring to the previous drawing, we see how the different length and angle of the control arms affects camber change. I have exaggerated the angle changes for illustration, but the effect is very real, as you'll know if you have ever had a car slip just a couple degrees out of alignment. All the drawings illustrate a car coming toward you while making a left hand turn. The body will roll outside of the turn, which is toward the left in the drawings.

The earliest Independent Front Suspensions were seen in the late '30s to early '50s. We discussed these earlier in this chapter as the Kingpin IFS design. These typically used a two piece spindle consisting of

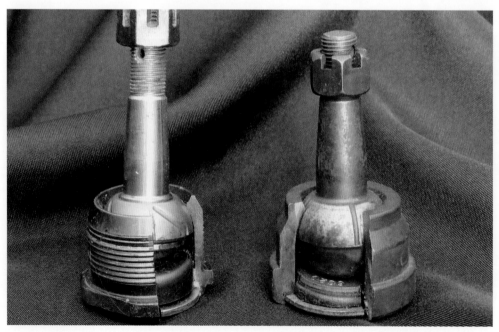

Sectioning and examining a 1969 Chevelle and threaded MOPAR ball joint as commonly used on fabricated MII control arms established the fact that there is no practical difference in their construction or suitability as use with a weight bearing lower control arm.

Wm. Longyard

54

the spindle proper carrying the wheel bearings, a vertical upright connecting the control arms thru pivot shafts and bushings, and swiveling for steering through a kingpin. These are actually quite good suspensions in most cases, with generally good geometry and little or no bumpsteer - with the notable exception of the '49-'51 Ford and '39-'48 Chevy IFS, which we analyzed in that earlier section of this chapter.

Referring to our drawing, we can see that as the body rolls and the frame-mount pivot points are therefore altered, the outer wheel does the right thing by going to negative camber, leaning into the turn like a bicycle or your Harley. The

inner wheel isn't helping us much since it is also going negative, but now leaning out of the turn. We have effectively lost nearly half of our front contact patch and will experience understeer, or "push" as you hear it on TV racing shows. Our situation is worsened as the geometry change also moves the center of gravity outboard.

The second set of drawings illustrate a more modern, but actually worse type design seen on many of our favorite musclecars. The upper control arms going downhill to the wheel creates a more limited down travel (bad for drag racers, you remember those now-outlawed upper ball joint spacers, right?) but more importantly caus-

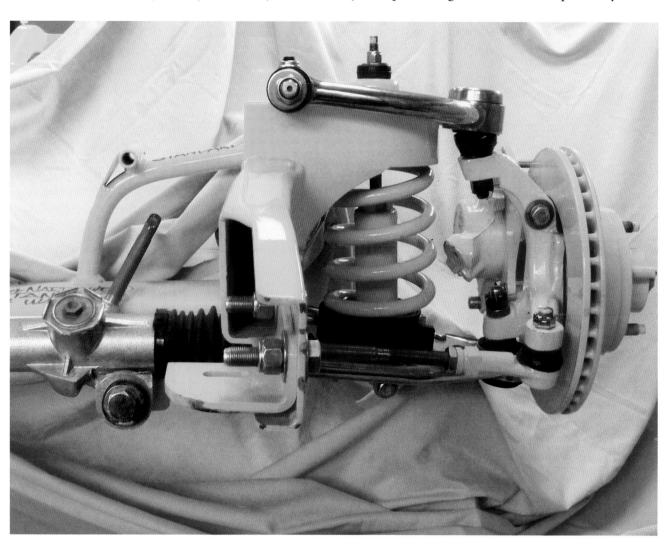

The basic MII IFS kit today will include tubular control arms, a standard type coil spring with an internally mounted shock absorber, steering system and spindles with brakes. Beware of brake systems that use undersize rotors and calipers as critical stopping power will be compromised.

es both tires to do the wrong thing. As you can see, they both lean out of the turn, the outer wheel going positive and the inner negative. Watch an early Chevelle or first-gen ('67-'69) Camaro try to corner hard and you'll see the inner tire trying very hard to reach the ground.

It's important to understand very clearly that positive or negative change itself is not the issue, but rather how that change relates to the side you are referring to and how that change affects the tire's contact patch. The center of gravity also hurts us by moving outboard, further increasing body roll while the rolled/displaced inner arm pivots cause camber change. Upgraded anti-sway bars and shock absorbers are really effective on these cars since the offending body roll can be minimized. Those create stronger roll stiffness but ride and handling suffer since the tire is less able to follow the road contour. Understeer is very strong since both tires are riding on the edge of the tread. You have heard of racers measuring temperature across the tread in order to understand how their contact patch is working. We would expect to see very hot temps on the side of the tires on the outboard side of the turn.

We must stop for a moment to explain a conflict in terminology that can create confusion in our discussion. When speaking to an oval track racer they generally refer to what is happening to the inner front tire (possibly since in oval track racing the outer tire tends to get plenty of traction due to weight transfer). Since the ideal thing is to have the inner wheel lean into the corner they will refer to this as positive camber gain. Road racers have to turn both

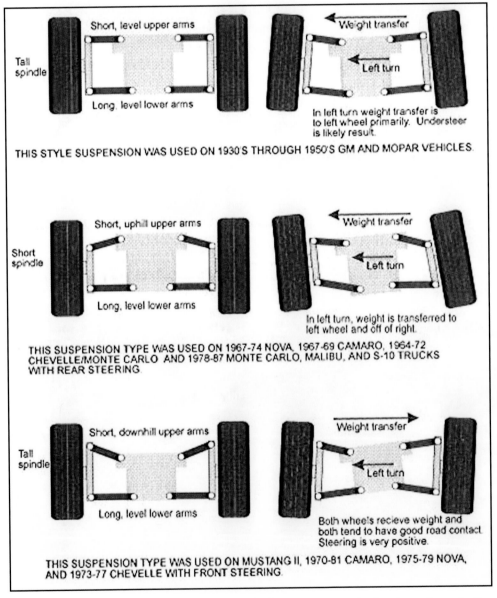

THIS STYLE SUSPENSION WAS USED ON 1930'S THROUGH 1950'S GM AND MOPAR VEHICLES.

THIS SUSPENSION TYPE WAS USED ON 1967-74 NOVA, 1967-69 CAMARO, 1964-72 CHEVELLE/MONTE CARLO AND 1978-87 MONTE CARLO, MALIBU, AND S-10 TRUCKS WITH REAR STEERING.

THIS SUSPENSION TYPE WAS USED ON MUSTANG II, 1970-81 CAMARO, 1975-79 NOVA, AND 1973-77 CHEVELLE WITH FRONT STEERING.

One can easily see how IFS design has evolved over time, and why the taller spindle concept with inwardly raked upper control arms offers superior road holding. It's always all about keeping the maximum tire tread on the ground at all times!

left and right and often refer to negative camber gain, this time applied to the outer wheel. Whatever it's called, they are really talking about the same concept where we want both wheels to lean into the turn, the ideal situation having the inner wheel go positive camber and the outer negative.

The third type can be very clearly seen on any Indy car. You will always see a long level lower arm and a shorter upper arm running uphill to the spindle. The front steer '70-'81 Camaros, Mustang II, and many custom IFS systems exhibit this geometry. Both wheels camber in the proper direction to maximize the contact patch as well as moving the center of gravity to the inside of the turn. That transferred CG position serves to lessen body roll as a bonus. Again, you hear this referred to as both, "positive and negative camber gain geometry." Both terms are correct, according to which wheel you are referring to. Note that this geometry is achieved by using a taller spindle than seen on the earlier musclecars. The taller

This appears to be a custom home made IFS system with very good design. The control arm and coil-over angles will provide good handling and ride, while the rack and pinion height and steering arms layout looks to exhibit good Ackerman and anti-bumpsteer control. The rod end control arm pivots may be a bit more noisy than urethane bushing but good maintenance will keep that from being a problem.

spindle also allows a larger "window" of suspension travel before topping or bottoming.

This type suspension is the norm in any advanced suspension design I have ever seen. In fact, the taller spindle concept is used on Mercedes Benz, NASCAR Cup chassis, Mustang II based IFS, and the C-4 and later Corvette. When very large diameter wheels are used the ball joints are occasionally located on the spindle itself and then pick up tapered holes in the ends of the control arms to get the maximum height ball joint separation. That yields even better results than in our traditional ball joints in the arms systems, but does require those very large wheel diameters.

I first became aware of this idea from an article in HOT ROD magazine from about 1973. Hotchkiss developed a kit to put the taller Second Gen ('70-'81) Camaro spindle on the First-gen ('64-'72) Chevelles. A special length upper control arm and modified lower ball joint

were required but this simple swap achieved a measured 20% improvement is skid pad numbers. Since both cars are front steer this worked out great, but could not be applied to the rear steer first-gen Camaros without creating major Ackerman problems. For whatever reason, this brilliant bit of hot rod engineering didn't really catch on until we started looking at hot rod handling as well as acceleration.

At Fatman Fab, we were selling dropped spindles for the First-gen Chevelle and First-gen ('67-'69) Camaro that had the downside of using the smaller Metric brakes and stock geometry. They were the best available at the time, but all they did was lower the car. In 2004 I began the design of a new dropped spindle that did more than just lower the car. The new design used the larger OEM disc brakes (as well as any aftermarket upgrade) and the taller height of the second- gen Camaro spindle. Since the First-gen Camaro and Chevelle share the same spindle with different bolt-on steering arms, it is possible to use the new spindle on either car by using their correct (and different) steering arms. I did have to relocate the tapered hole for the upper ball joint to allow the use of standard length control arms, but that actually improved the scrub radius with wider wheels. An analysis of possible bumpsteer showed that since the upper control arm angle-change affected the steering arc, a lowered steering arm position was needed to achieve minimized

Comparison of the stock versus taller and dropped spindle for First Gen Camaro and Chevelle shows how the superior positive camber gain geometry exhibited by their Second Generation cousins can be transplanted with amazing improvement in handling ability and little expense or trouble.

bumpsteer. We got the drop, better brakes and vastly improved handling with a simple bolt-on part.

After introducing the new spindle to the hot rod market, I found out that I had rediscovered a concept that had been around NASCAR since the sixties! Some of you may know that until the 1980s NASCAR's IFS design was essentially a beefed up version of the '57-'64 full sized Fords (similar to how the modern hot rod Mustang II IFS has been improved). I was watching the "American Pickers" TV show when they went to Pete Pistone's shop right here in Charlotte. He showed Mike and Frank a '57-'64

stock Ford spindle that had been modified by welding on a gusseted and raised upper ball joint mod. The same concept was used when the '67-'69 Penske Trans Am Camaros also swapped to the taller Corvette spindle for this reason, along with their larger brakes. I remember reading that they had a little trouble getting their necessary special length upper arms past the tech inspectors, since those guys thought it was about weight savings rather than enhanced handling. Back then the guys often lacked the benefit of an engineering education, but their amazing common sense often told them the same things!

This IFS has been plated with the electroless nickel process, which is far less expensive and troublesome than conventional chrome plating. It is a great option for an IFS that stays good looking with minimal effort.

Wm. Longyard

This idea of getting the improved upper control arm angle can also be achieved by the "Guldstrand Mod" for First-gen Camaros and Chevelles and the "Shelby Mod" for Mustangs where the inner mount of the upper arm is lowered. Racers now can choose special ball joints with taller studs to achieve the same benefits. You cannot achieve this incredibly important effect with tubular control arms that have differently curved tubes but don't alter the ball joint position. That's marketing, not engineering.

If I had a First-gen Camaro or Chevelle this would be my first step toward enhanced suspension performance. Lowering the CG and transferring it inboard in a turn and maximizing tire traction will allow your better, wider tires and brakes to perform at the best of their ability. Stock springs and control arm bushings in good shape will work fine. Shocks and sway bars can be upgraded without resorting to such gonzo rates that your CD player skips. It will be capable of putting in respectable Autocross numbers without having to become a race car. By fixing the REAL design problem FIRST, you'll have a much better handling car that is fun to drive on the road.

McPherson Strut IFS

The McPherson strut IFS is another type of IFS that has become very popular. This concept was pioneered in Europe and is still used on many of their finest cars such as the Porsche and BMW. When first introduced to the U.S. market it was used on smaller cars that emulated the fuel-efficient smaller cars so common in Europe. Unfortunately, this connection to what were perceived as gas crisis relevant economy cars with indifferent build quality common in the 1980's seems to have led to a prejudice against McPherson strut systems in American performance cars. When critical positive design features such as good camber control for maximum tire patch, minimized bumpsteer, minimized unsprung weight, and more space for

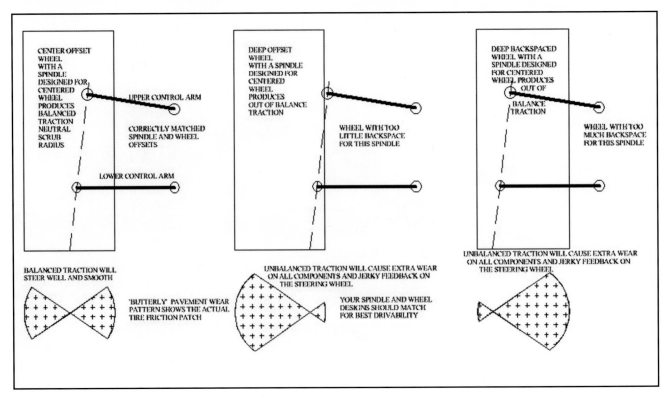

Proper wheel offset is specific to the spindle being used on that suspension. If an incorrect wheel offset is used, the tire's traction will become unbalanced causing strange handling and loss of traction, particularly in a tight turn.

wide engines in narrow cars, the strut IFS actually looks pretty good. Perhaps that is why the '79 up Mustang and fifth gen (2010 and up) Camaro designers have gone to this design.In this design the shock strut is constructed with enough rigidity so that the upper control arm is no longer needed to control the wheel camber. That can save a lot of engine bay space so that engines and exhaust can be fitted into narrower cars, than with double A-arm IFS designs. The coil spring can be mounted on either the lower control arm or the strut body itself with a coil-over type design. Aftermarket conversions typically use the coil-over design and add an adjustable lower spring seat to add a feature of tunable ride height. Rack and pinion and disc brakes are pretty much universal features with this type of suspension.

Another subtle advantage of this design is that they have a very high roll center. On the surface that sounds bad until we remember that it is the RELATIONSHIP between roll center (RC) and center of gravity (CG) that creates body roll. CG on most cars will be very close to camshaft height on the average V-8 engine. If the roll center is lower than that in most double A-arm IFS designs, body roll to the outside of the corner will develop. That will require fairly stiff anti-sway bars to keep body roll under control. The high CG with strut IFS actually wants to roll the car into a turn so minimal sway bars are required. The beauty of this feature is bet-

ter ride quality, and tire-to-road adhesion because the suspension by requiring less stiff suspension components.

All the above advantages and remarkably similar layout and dimensions make strut IFS a very attractive swap option for the unibody Ford compacts of the Sixties. Read that as: '60-'71 Falcon, '65-'73 Mustang, '62-'71 Fairlane/Torino, and of course the Mercury variants of those very popular cars. The strut IFS fits very well, being generally a bolt-in situation while space for engine exhaust is maximized. Even more important is the fact that the car weight is carried into the shock towers just as the original engineers at Ford envisioned. Adjustable ride height, improved rack and pinion steering and better handling are additional advantages.

Upgrades to cars designed for strut IFS as well as swap kits would include better shocks, sway bars and upgraded brakes which will be discussed in later chapters.

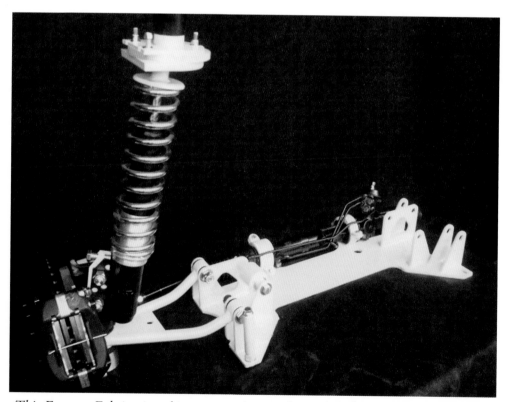

This Fatman Fabrications kit converts the popular early Falcons, Mustangs and Fairlanes to a far superior IFS system from the '94-'04 Mustang for transformed drivability in a bolt in no weld package.

Chapter Five

Independent Suspension Swaps

Almost too many Options

Many rodders will be building cars that came with a workable factory IFS system. Whether the early kingpin type, classic fifties, muscle car or even the later pickups, a wide assortment of upgrades are available to lower the vehicle, improve handling and upgrade braking. For some of those the best solution can be to replace the factory IFS completely with a new IFS – it's often much easier to do, costs less, or simply offers more advancement than modifying

This well sorted 1966 Chevelle chassis has all the bells and whistles! Improved power steering, tall dropped spindles, tubular arms with improved geometry, advanced brakes, trick sway bar and a high end shock and coil-over conversion combine to provide performance and ride quality that will rival any modern performance car..

the original suspension. Builders of earlier rods that came factory equipped with solid axle suspension will often start with a brand new IFS rather than trying to improve on what that solid axle suspension can offer. The variety of vehicle types, and available IFS upgrades, is such a wide topic as to make covering all the considerations nearly impossible - certainly so in the space of this book. So in order to help the rodder decide which option is best for his particular combination of skills, equipment, level of expected performance and style, or the ever present budget, let's look at the various option as they have appeared in the sport.

SWAP OPTIONS

Some of the earliest IFS conversions involved using the '49-'54 Chevy IFS. These unbolt from the donor car and can be bolted back into a '39-'48 Chevy without too much trouble. They can also be welded into some other cars when the frame rail dimensions are compatible. Pluses are the very fact that they are an IFS and that since they share most parts with the '53-'62 Corvette IFS, the aftermarket has plenty of lowering, shock and brake upgrades to offer. Down sides would include the somewhat

This 1959 Ford retractable will be a thoroughly modern hot rod with the Fatman Fab front IFS stub, Ridetech shocks waves all around, and a supercharged 5.4 from a wrecked Shelby Mustang. A new 9" Ford rear with a matching Ridetech triangulated 4 bar, Shockwaves, disc brakes and sway bar complete the chassis upgrade. Wm. Longyard

This blown Ford 5.4 engine will be a real performer, and with the upgraded brakes and steering it will be capable of using that power safely. Adding a lot of power without proper attention and upgrading of the chassis can cause the car to become a hazard on the road. Wm. Longyard

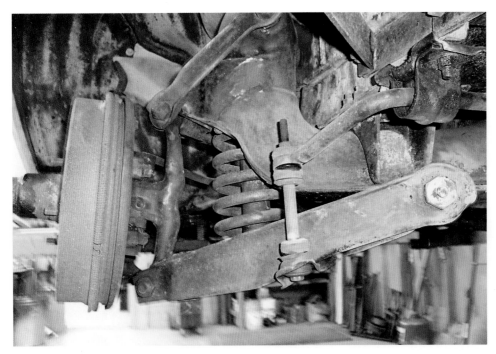

The '49-'54 Chevy was good enough to be used on the Corvette from '53-'62, and can be upgraded in several ways. Most modern rodders choose however to replace it with a MII or new Corvette IFS rather than trying to improve an already dated design.

A typical MII hub to hub kit will include the crossmember, steering, control arms, springs and shocks along with spindles and brakes. Later the steering connections and plumbing will be added to complete the installation.

antiquated kingpin IFS design with limited caster settings and less convenient parts access than for more modern IFS systems. Basically, since we are using an IFS that many people choose to replace in the original donor car, this option has pretty much faded away.

The Corvair IFS was quite popular in the Street Rod revival era in the 1970s. Its bolt-in design can be handy and it will fit under Model A type fenders reasonably well. Downsides are the short spindle, negative-camber-gain geometry discussed in the last chapter as being less than ideal, and the common practice of converting these IFS to rack and pinion steering. The Corvair was a front steer design, which often interfered with radiator lower splash shields, causing many rodders to change to a rear-steer rack by reversing the spindles. Then rodders began swapping ball joints to install First-gen Camaro and Chevelle spindles to get disc brakes and stronger parts. This created Ackerman problems and often bumpsteer simply because few rodders then understood proper design geometry. Most of these IFS have since been replaced as parts supplies have dried up and better designs evolved.

Early street rods with Model A style fenders (often referred to as open fender cars) often used a conversion coming from the Jaguar XKE roadsters. These will fit under the fenders well and the track width worked out about right. Various rear-steer rack and pinions were used with varying results according to how much bumpsteer occurred, but we soldiered on with these IFS as the hot rodders knowledge continued to advance. Advantages are disc brakes, adjustable ride height with torsion bars and trick styling especially when chromed. Problems included a fairly involved installation, necessary steering conversions and high cost. Again, although in favor for a time, they have faded into history. There were also some adventures into bolt-in OEM IFS such as the Volare and Pacer, but track width, ride height and dried up parts supplies have essentially caused their disappearance.

There was a huge swing into the fat fendered '35-'48 street rods in the late 1970s, one that continues to this day. Being a closed fender car, there developed a wide interest in using OEM IFS subframes, especially from the first-gen Camaro and its cousin the '68-'74 Nova. Gaining a modern IFS with ball joints, factory mounted power steering, and disc brakes made this a popular path to an IFS system. When the swap was well planned and performed, ride quality and handling gains were quite satisfactory. However, some installers did less than workmanlike fabrication, or got into trouble with too wide a track width, poor planning for final ride height, and difficulties

remounting the sheet metal and bumper. Although engine mounts were on the subframe, they often had to be relocated 3"-4" farther back, which led to extra work and a common problem finding a coil spring soft enough to work properly with the now lighter front end load.

As the early rear steer subframes got more scarce, partly due to the boom in restoring these cars, rodders began to use the second-gen '70-'81 Camaro subframes. These have far better geometry than the first-gen version, but wide track width and very wide and high forward frame rails led to many cars being left without front bumpers, while the forward position of the steering box was often a problem in clearing the car's original radiator core support. Dropped spindles, coil-overs and narrowed arms came on the market to help solve these problems. The later G body ('78-'87 Monte Carlo/Malibu etc.) and S-10 subframes are narrower but have the small bore Metric calipers known for marginal stop-

This 1940 Ford chassis has had a Fatman Fabrications MII IFS kit installed, along with a new X member and mounts for a Chevy small block engine and trans.

Here we see a Model A chassis with a custom coil-over IFS by Studley's Independent Chassis. The upper A arm mounts and rear steer rack make this a nice fit in the Model A.

ping power and also reverted to the first-gen type poor camber curve geometry, while having the forward steering box and frame rail position issues as the second-gen Camaro subframe. They seem to combine the worst features of both Camaro IFS types; their only virtue being narrower track width. All in all the subframe era seems to have come to the end of its road.

As the street rod hobby exploded in the 1980s, and rodders started driving far longer distances than ever before, many manufacturers saw the interest in IFS conversions along with the problems of the OEM based units just discussed. First, the MII IFS (based on '74-'78 Mustang II) was installed by cutting the crossmember out of the stock unibody structure then notching and welding it into the project car. The geometry is among the best, with a power steering rack option, and the installation offered much promise. Problems with clearing early open fenders, the front steer rack hitting splash shields, small disc brakes, a weak crossmember and track width issues quickly came to light. An entire

aftermarket segment came to life with fixes for the problems. In fact the MII IFS is that only in name as every single component has been made available in reproduction.

New spindles made in dropped, stock and even raised versions make it easy to tune the ride height to your personal taste. Control arms in tubular steel or stainless in different track widths and schemes for mounting stock coil springs, coilovers, and Air Ride are readily available. Sway bars and special height outer tie rod ends improve handling, while the improved brake kits could fill a chapter all by themselves. (Be cautious with designs that require special length outer tie rod ends as bumpsteer often results.) Heavy wall crossmembers, stronger control arms and ball joints handle the strength issues for cars up to 4,000 pounds. Ride height and track width can be altered, without creating geometry problems, for excellent fit on an amazing variety of cars and trucks. Given the upgrades, versatility, affordability and now endlessly assured parts pipeline, the MII IFS seems to be here to stay.

Cars which have a coil spring pocket integral with the frame rail were often subframed in the past. Done right they work very well but track width and refitting the sheet metal can be problematic. Now you can purchase either specific fit-per-application, or universal IFS subframes based on the MII or Corvette IFS which can be installed in these cars. A less "Frankenstein" frame joint is often the result while ride height and track width can be tailored per your application. The specific fit type will also offer reproduced mounts for the sheet metal and front bumper while the universal type requires "you" to figure out those details. Some rodders with good fabrication abilities choose to build their own rectangular tubing front rails and then add IFS to that. In any case, this is a far easier, albeit sometimes slightly more expensive, alternative to a Camaro subframe swap that has really taken over in the fifties car market.

With the advent of the C4 Corvette in 1984, rodders were attracted to the all aluminum construction of the control arms and spindles along with a bolt-in-design crossmember that even mounted the power rack and pinion. In the right car these work extremely well, such as the '55-'57 Chevy. Track width can be a problem on many cars as this is a quite wide IFS. It is also very important that a wheel with the factory backspace offset be used to preserve the correct scrub radius (which we will discuss in the chapter on

In order to widen the MII track width for this 1967 F100, a 4" long rack main shaft extension is added to space out the right hand inner tie rod end. The lower control arm inner pivot mounts were also moved 4" further apart than stock. By using a single 4" extension on the passenger side, the extra benefit of moving the U joint connection shaft 2" further from the engine is achieved, ion the interest of better header clearance.

This 2" dropped spindle is fabricated using CNC processes for strength and accuracy. It allows users of the Volare/Aspen, Cordoba, and many other MOPAR IFS systems to get the car down lower without having to wind down the torsion bars and lose suspension travel.

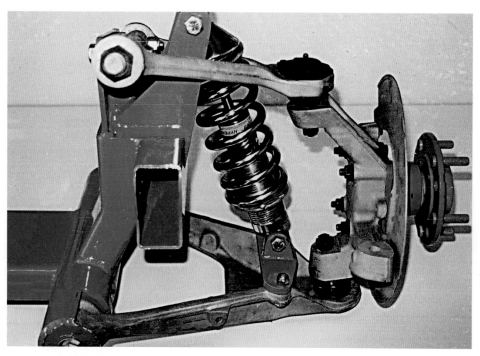

Most Corvette IFS conversions will include a change to coil-overs rather than the original transverse fiberglass spring. This not only cleans up the IFS considerably but makes it much easier to get the correct spring rate for the vehicle.

wheel selection) and keep the track width as stock. Using a more normal centered offset wheel will result in an even wider track width but more importantly the tire will scrub sideways rather than rolling smoothly thru a tight turn angle. That skidding loss of traction will degrade brake and handling performance not to mention creating an embarrassing squeal in a parking lot. Aftermarket crossmembers generally go to a coil-over conversion to make it easier to match spring weights to the new home of the Vette IFS. Another issue is that at the same ride height the Corvette rack and pinion will be about 2" higher in the chassis than a MII conversion, so that can be a problem if your engine sits forward in the chassis. The C4 Corvette IFS is an excellent option for many cars as long as the rack height, track width and wheel selection issues are fully considered.

The aftermarket has continued to evolve with scratch built new IFS designs, some actually based in MII geometry, custom spindles or the use of C4 Corvette spindles and/or control arms. Special tubular control arms and coil-over conversions are typical of this approach. Clever design can make these rear steer

This 1968 Ford F100 has had a 1996 Ford Crown Victoria IFS swapped. The installation is quite simple with a good fit to the stock frame rails and only a rear mount for the lower control arms needing to be fabbed. However, this front end is 7" wider than the typical F100 so wheel fitment is going to be a real problem. It is not possible to make narrowed control arms, so it is perhaps fortunate that these swaps tend to have a conservative ride height when finished.

for use in early open fender cars. Track width and ride height can be dialed in per the application while correct geometry is typically retained. Those aftermarket designs using C4-C6 Corvette spindles generally have a special steering arm, which lowers the rack to help with engine clearance issues - while most adapt a late model Mustang power rack to allow narrowing the track width a bit. These can be a superb IFS design although the use of all new design parts and high-end brakes can make them pricey.

Pickup trucks from 1955 up with OEM solid axles and generally straight rails present a slightly different approach. Their track width is also greater than many cars so options like the GM subframes and Corvette IFS find more acceptance in this market. MII based IFS can be made wider to fit very well but it is important to be sure that the widening is done properly. If the IFS is widened in the center (control arms mounted further apart than stock MII) then the rack must be wider at its inner pivots as well, typically by using a machined rack extension that moves the inner tie rod ends inside the rack boots further apart. Widening can also be accomplished correctly by keeping the steering and control arm inner pivots in their stock position and then using longer than stock outer tie rod ends and control arms to push the wheels outboard. Either method will work, but widening the suspension in the middle and the steering on the outer end is a sure-fire recipe for creating massive bumpsteer. Given the variety of options, widths and easy installation the MII IFS has proven very popular for these trucks.

The Volare bolt in IFS used to be popular, but as mentioned, parts availability has slowed that way down. Ride height can be a problem on existing installations though dropped spindles are available that allow the torsion bars to be wound back up to recover lost suspension and shock travel. A well-done subframe installation can do a good job on these trucks as well if the width, ride height and body mounting issues are handled correctly.

We do see and hear about the '82-'93 S-10 complete chassis being used under hot rod pickups, but the primary advantage seems to be they are cheap with so many rusted out S-10s out there. There was no V-8 option so engine mounts have to be made. The track width is so narrow that the rear end typically has to be changed, and either special LONGER control arms or 3" per side wheel spacers used to get the wheels where they belong. At least the wheelbase is OK for most pickups, being at 115". Then there is a problem with the front-mount steering box interfering with many radiator core supports and the need for quite a few adaptor brackets

Here is a nicely detailed S-10 chassis that has had the adaptor brackets added to allow a '55-'59 Chevy PU cab and bed to be installed. Not easily seen are the 3" wheel spacers needed to extend the track to put the tires in fenders properly.

This early Mustang has had the McPherson strut from the '94-'04 Mustang bolted in using a kit form Fatman Fabrications. IT offers simple installation, better steering and brakes, adjustable ride height, and adherence to Ford unibody design and the way that the car's weight is intended to be carried. The complete lack of an upper control arm allows the shock towers to be trimmed for header clearance but do not require that mod if the installer prefers to leave the car uncut.

Wm. Longyard

bought or made to remount the bumper, cab, and bed. With the original frames being flat on top and the S-10 having a deep middle drop those brackets can get a little agricultural in style. But they are cheap.

The 1993 up Crown Victoria IFS has been getting a lot of attention, especially as it all mounts on an aluminum one-piece crossmember that easily bolts into a 34" outside width frame rail common to the '53-'79 F100 and '55-'59 Chevy PU. The only fab work is drilling some holes and making a simple mount for the rear of the lower control arm. Geometry and brakes are good, the cop versions having bigger rotors mounted on aluminum spindles and control arms. The big problem is that their 68" hub-to-hub track width conflicts badly with the original truck's need for a 61"-62" track width to keep the tires under the fenders. Since the Crown Vic IFS is about 7" too wide (3 ½" per side) you are going to need a wheel with a very deep backspace that looks like it came from a front wheel drive car. We are talking about something along the lines of an 8" wide wheel with 7" of back space!

Fatman's IFS installed here on their own 1967 F100 shop truck. It has given years of service as a normal shop truck and pulling trailers across the country. The Shockwaves work great to carry variable loads while the track width matches the original for excellent tire clearance, especially as compared to the Crown Vic IFS seen earlier.

That is not most people's idea of a pretty wheel. It won't be an easy wheel to find in many styles and the extreme scrub radius imbalance may cause some serious drivability issues. There is no room to narrow the factory control arms, and narrowing the crossmember would require a new or modified rack AND the easy-bolt-on-to-the-standard-frame width advantage goes away. If one is keeping the truck at a conservative ride height you may be OK, but low trucks are going to have problems with wheel to fender clearance.

If you have a 1960 and later GM pickup the market is full of companies making suspension parts. For most rodders a simple pair of dropped disc brake spindles, new lowered or one-coil-cut original springs will get you a 4" drop. Add some lowered rear coil springs or lowering blocks on the leaf rear-spring trucks and you are all set. If you are going lower than a 4" drop a problem will crop up with minimal front ground clearance with the lower control arm inner pivots. There is a raised crossmember kit that lowers the truck while gaining the necessary clearance, or you can replace the suspension entirely with one of several kits that bolt in like the original and set the truck lower and also gain about 3" of ground clearance. These will also have a cleaner hot rod style and offer endless options of spring type including Air Ride and brake options.

This bolt-in replacement IFS for the '60-'87 GM pickups adds style, better steering and brakes, but the real advantages are more ground and tire clearance for really low trucks.

Chapter Six

Rear Suspension

Solid Axle - or IRS

The rear suspension on our hot rods has two primary jobs: to support the weight of the back of the vehicle, and to control the position of the wheels relative to how the chassis goes down the highway. Independent rear suspension is more complicated and less common than a solid rear axle, so we'll deal with that later in this chapter.

Solid rear axle suspension is often called "live axle", and has to keep the axle square in the car so that a tendency to turn is not induced. You certainly would not intentionally install a rear suspension out of square, but that often happens accidentally due to improper design or installation.

Corvette IRS rear suspension swaps have been popular for years with their good looks and anticipated ride and handling improvements. Modern improvements have enhanced their functionality while some of the fit and installation difficulties remain.

VanSteel

Leaf spring suspension is commonly used on hot rods and will always be the most simple and cost effective design. Properly designed and installed, it easily positions the rear axle and supports the weight of the car. The Early Fords (1904-48) used single transverse springs fore and aft, which worked pretty well in the days of unpaved roads and lightweight cars. As road speed and car weight increased, the necessarily stronger springs had to be stiffened - to the detriment of ride quality. Ford switched to the parallel leaf arrangement, so common today, in 1949, and most other manufacturers have used this design from the beginning.

With the proper leaf count and traction aid arrangement, applied torque at the rear wheels can be controlled, up to a point. This type of arrangement can be easily lowered or raised according to the builder's wishes. Since the leaves have to absorb the energy of the car's weight along with engine torque, they can reach a point

This 1948 Ford original chassis has had a dual leaf spring rear suspension from Chassis Engineering installed along with their shocks, sway bar and an 8" Ford rear axle. This is a simple and cost effective great driving arrangement which works well in a great many hot rod projects.

A new '37-'39 Chevy chassis by Fatman features very similar components as seen on the '34-'48 Ford swaps. Note the rear anti-sway bar mounted inside the chassis to provide clearance for the calipers on a rear disc brake set up. Exhaust pipe clearance is also improved with this design.

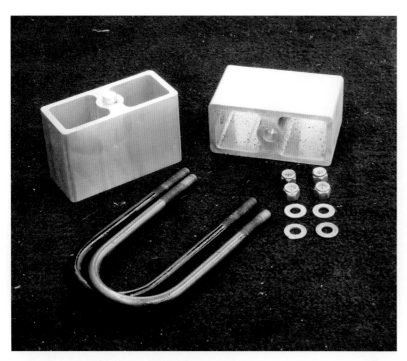

A simple lowering block set provides an easy way to fine tune your final ride height without altering the spring rate. Keep them at 2" tall maximum to avoid problems with pinion rise under acceleration. These can also be a real problem solver if you need to alter your rear axle position to better center the tire in the fender.

Wm. Longyard

where the energy exceeds the spring's ability to handle it. That is a scientific way of saying that too much weight and traction creates an overload of energy that is released as spring wrap up and wheel hop. Adding the right shock absorbers, sway bar, and traction aids will provide excellent performance. We will discuss those springs, shocks and sway bars in separate chapters so let's deal with the geometry involved in rear suspension traction in this chapter.

A more complex type of rear suspension involving radius rods, (or "bars" as termed today) will have some type of bar arrangement that positions the axle fore and aft as well as sideways. Unlike a leaf spring arrangement in which the springs have to absorb the energy of torque reaction at the wheels along with the weight of the car, the bars only have to position the axle and are naturally more resistant to wheel hop. With the springs no longer loaded with drivetrain torque and only handling the car weight, lower rate springs can be used with enhanced ride and handling as the result.

The most common type of rear four-bar has been the equal length parallel type. When viewed from the side or the top the bars will be essentially parallel to each other, with small variations not uncommon or necessarily problematic. The bars are generally threaded on at least one end to allow for adjustment, with double threaded LH/RH ends allowing easier length adjustment with the bar still bolted in place on

The venerable Early Ford transverse rear spring can be made to work very well by fine tuning the spring leaves, and really puts out that vintage vibe. In this case it is also essential to allow clearance for that quick change rear axle assembly.

the chassis. Urethane or rubber-end-bushed rod ends are preferred since the all-metal swivel ball bearing rod ends (often called Heim ends after the name of a major manufacturer) tend to rattle and wear quickly on the street. The mounts for the bars on the frame and axle can be arranged to be adjustable to allow fine-tuning of this type suspension. A common problem with this ideal equal length system is that the upper bars often interfere with floors on production cars. That interference can generally be relieved by pockets added to the floor, which hide under the back seat, this may still be a very good way to go.

Sideways movement with a four-bar must be controlled with some sort of separate device. In fact it might better be referred to these systems as a five-bar to differentiate it from other rear control systems. The most common transverse control has been the Panhard bar, which simply mounts one end to the frame (generally on the driver side) and the other to the axle. It should be as long and level as possible to minimize lateral movement of the axle as it moves up and down.

This '37 Ford has a Posies rear leaf kit installed. It will sit lower than other kits yet tucks up into the frame for a clean appearance under the running-boards. It uses 1 ¾" wide rear leafs to help accomplish this, with extra leaves to do the same work as wider leaves seen in other kits. Some body styles will need floor mods to fit the forward spring perch.

Fatman Fab's '35-'40 Ford display chassis was built to show rear suspensions could be different type of rear suspension. The right side is a good example of how a parallel 4 bar is generally arranged. Not shown is the lateral locator bar that would be needed in a real installation.

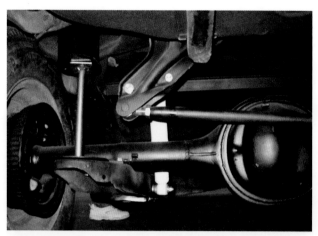

This 1939 Buick has received a 9" rear axle swap with airsprings. The vertical set up bar at far left assures that the upper airspring mount is at the correct height while the lower mount bolts in just like the original coil spring. A new adjustable Panhard bar makes recentering the axle with changing ride height simple.

The '39 Buick trailing arms are boxed for strength as they now have to resist the axle rotation formerly resisted by the now gone torque tube. Reuse the original Buick trailing arms axle mounts and add some tube shocks from the front of a '73-'87 Chevy PU and you have a suspension much like used in NASCAR to this day.

Adjustable length will be important to fine-tune the centering of the axle. The position of the Panhard bar over the axle can be a problem when fitting exhaust tailpipes, so other options are sometimes a better choice.

The "Z" bar is an interesting variation that eliminates the over axle exhaust problem by being mounted to the front left and right rear corner of the four-bar. If driveshaft clearance will allow, it is best mounted on the upper bars to create a slightly higher roll center for less body roll. Since that is often a problem, mounting it to the lower bars will work fine but creates the need for a little more rear roll stiffness, although in the real world very little affect is noted. Double LH/RH threads are almost always used to make centering the axle easy. This time ½" spherical rod ends are commonly used with good results. A fairly new innovation in hot rodding, it has long been in use on drag cars.

A further variation is the Watts link, which is a much more complicated way of locating the rear axle side to side. With at least 5 pivot points, two bars and a fairly large center bracket this design adds quite a bit of unsprung weight…never a good thing. It truly only keeps the rear axle centered in the middle of its travel when the bars are level. Given the complexity and weight it has fallen out of favor as being overkill engineering for any street oriented design.

Another variation on the four-bar is the four-link, commonly used for drag racing. It uses upper and lower bars that are seldom parallel, or even the same length. Both ends of the bars can be raised or lowered in order to tune the system, changing the "bite" according to track conditions. What's really happening is that we have an adjustable length ladder bar system. If you make an imaginary line that extends the bars forward, those lines will eventually cross at a point called the instant center. As the angle of the bars are altered, that instant center can be moved up and down to change rear chassis rise, and forward or back to alter the weight transfer. All that is fine for a drag racer, but it doesn't answer the challenges of a street car as well as a more typical four-bar. It also tends to take up a great deal more space so you will often see the trunk area minimized or eliminated. It can be readjusted to have the bars level for the street and altered for drag racing, so it can work well for a dual-purpose hot rod.

We've been discussing equal length four-bars here, since that is the ideal for normal road use. You can also get good results from a four-bar which has shorter upper bars to fit under a floor which you'd rather not cut to clear equal length bars. There will be an increasing amount of pinion angle change as the difference in bar length increases, so watch using too short a bar length. Given the limited suspension travel available from coil-overs with only 4"-5" of travel, pinion change has not proven to be a problem.

Turning on the opinion warning light, I would be very leery of an upper bar less than 70% of the lower bar length. You will still need a sideways, lateral locating device as just discussed for a parallel four-bar.

Triangulated rear 4 bars can work very well, especially with Air Ride. You see this design in many aftermarket rear axle systems as well as on factory cars like the '64-'72 Chevelle which have rear coil springs. They do have a shorter upper bar since it is angled to provide lateral axle location without the use of a Panhard bar. The working length of that bar would not be its actual measured length, but rather the effective length as seen in a side view. That shorter upper should still be true level and parallel to the lower bar for best handling. In some

Greater range of adjustability is a major factor is the use of this design. By varying the angles of the bars, a tuner can alter the traction characteristics of the suspension, much like having a variable length ladder bar would operate. They find most use in dual street/drag applications but look so good and fit so well, particularly for pick up applications, that they get installed and may never make use of that tenability for traction.

This design first came into wide usage with the advent of coil rear suspension on cars like the First Gen Chevelle. They also work particularly well with Airride rear suspension by offering space for the airspring as well as very free articulation for enhanced ride and handling qualities. Wm. Longyard applications this different mounting makes more room for exhaust, better floor pan clearance, or a perfect spot to mount coil springs or air springs. Drivability is excellent, as good as a "five-bar". The only real downside is that they are designed to mount to a weldable axle housing, so guys with 10/12 bolt, Dana, and Ford 8.8 axles, may have a problem. Don't think that you can use some magic rod to weld suspension parts to cast iron axle housings!

Yet another variation on the four-bar is the 3 Link which come out of oval track racing. The idea is that a central bar can be longer and still clear the floor since it can "hide" in the drive-shaft tunnel, if there is enough extra space there. The greater length matched to the rear bars is a geometric advantage but the needed extra space is often just not available. Because of the space problem, a very similar type of third link was

used on the '58-'70 Chevy full size car. That center link being pretty short was the cause of more pinion angle change than seen on other designs. On a car that heavy it is questionable just how well the three-bar was able to control lateral axle travel.

A further variation of the 3 bar is the torque link. Just as in the 3 bar, two lower bars are used to control the fore and aft position of the axle along with a transverse location bar as just discussed. The upper center bar is then replaced with a long truss structure that fastens rigidly to the front of the axle housing and is able to take up any axle pinion rise. The forward end of that torque link bar is then mounted to the chassis near the forward driveshaft U joint. That forward mount must have a sliding or pivoting design to make up for length change since it moves in a different arc length than the lower bars. Traction

This triangulated four link provides transverse axle location by creating a triangular relationship between the frame, axle housing, and upper and lower bars. The shorter upper bars work very well in clearing the floor of cars with a rear seat pan that makes longer bars impractical, yet traction control has proven to be excellent in practice.

Wm. Longyard

78

and handling are excellent but it is a relatively heavy system that needs a fair bit of space to fit without interfering with the floor.

Then there is the trailing arm system as first seen on the 1960s Chevy pickups. Modern versions of this kit include bolt-in upgrades fabricated from round or square tubing to save weight, increase torsional rigidity and improve appearance. Very long arms are mounted rigidly to the rear axle housing to control torque and then run forward to a crossmember usually near the forward driveshaft U-joint. The bars also run inboard as they go forward, which allows rear suspension movement and rotation to go over road bumps. Notice how similar this is to the vintage Ford and GM torque tube/wishbone suspension.

Early Fords in the Flathead era were commonly set up with a late model rear axle mounted on radius rods salvaged from another Early Ford torque tube rear axle. Then the radius rods were spilt and mounted to the side of the frame rails with tie rod ends, much like the traditional front split wishbone. This design also suffers from the roll resistance created as the radius rods being split to the frame and trying to twist the axle housing or break parts whichever came first. A very few early rodders understood that problem and kept the forward mounting point very near the centerline of the

A rear four in this case uses a "Z" bar to accomplish the triangulation that keeps the rear axle centered regardless of axle vertical movement. While Panhard bars and Watts linkage often make exhaust routing over the axle very difficult, this design makes it simple with its low mounting.

We have held an additional bar in place on a parallel 4 bar to show how a 3 bar arrangement can be installed. As you can see, floor clearance will often be a real problem, which is why it sees more use on oval track Modified race cars than on hot rods. This is why the torque arm mounted under the rear axle has begun to see use on hot rods, although one then has to contend with ground clearance issues.
Wm. Longyard

This nicely arranged home built chassis features a parallel 4 bar with a shorter upper bar to clear the body. Given the 4" travel allowed by the coil-overs this works fine as the parallelism is more important than the length difference. An unseen Panhard bar handles sideways control.

car, thus freeing the rear suspension to articulate and better follow the road. As bigger tires and engines added to the torque applied to the rear axle, another problem cropped up when the welds and or brackets holding the radius rods to the axle housings began failing. In the original torque design the torque tube itself handled the pinion control force, which is why is it called a torque tube! The nice looking tapered rods we now are trying to use as radius rods controlling the axle were only designed to keep the axle square in the chassis…never having to accept the loads now placed on them.

As we are now building replicas and restoring vintage hot rods with more traction and torque, this problem is recurring. The joint between the axle housing should be reinforced and the vintage radius rods reinforced at that joint to help handle the torque. The bars will live longer and the suspension will work better if the forward ends of the radius rods are returned to a more wishbone like shape with the forward pivot bushings mounted as close to the car's centerline as possible. Aftermarket radius rods made much stronger than stock are available, as are kits using a fabricated tube radius rod that can take the torque, along with bracketry strong enough for the axle end and brought together up front for suspension to road compliance. If mounted with a transverse "buggy" spring per the

This '37-'39 Chevy chassis benefits from the use of a triangulated 4 bar to clear the floor and rear mounted fuel tank. The tail pipe installer's job is greatly eased with the 4 bar combined with an under axle mounted anti-sway bar.

Wm. Longyard

original Ford design, there may be no need for a lateral control bar. For improved control or the use of coil springs, coil-overs or Air Ride, a Panhard bar is typically used to control side-to-side movement of the axle.

Late '30s Olds and Buick cars that came with rear coil springs respond well to this design. In those cases the trailing arms

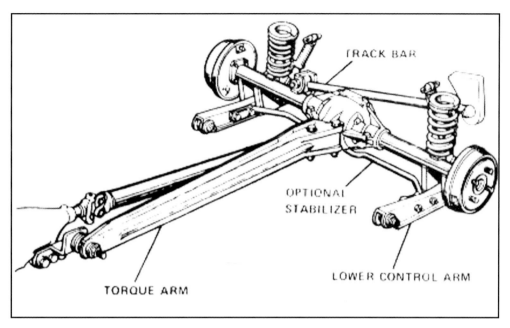

that originally mounted to the torque tube can be reinforced by boxing and then having their forward ends mounted to the frame rather than the torque tubes. This becomes in essence much like the early Ford design just discussed. With coil springs, coil-overs or Air Ride there remains a need to control axle movement side-to-side. The original Panhard bars and associated brackets can be transferred to the new rear axle housing. Add some tube shocks and a rear sway bar and a very economical yet effective rear suspension has

been built. The trailing link is fairly heavy but does provide very good traction, handling and ride quality. The biggest problem is that while pickups have plenty of room for this system under the bed floor, they are often hard to fit under a car with sunken rear footwells without hanging them too far under the car.

The old ladder bar traction aids that were added to both leaf and coil-spring suspensions

Torque arm suspension seems to be an evolution of the same theory as used with a 3 link, but this time the single central bar is solidly mounted to the axle housing and then mounted forward in a vertically limited but lengthwise sliding joint. The idea is that the more forward frame attach point provides better weight transfer for traction, as long as the space is available and the increase in unsprung weight doesn't "cost" more than the traction gain.

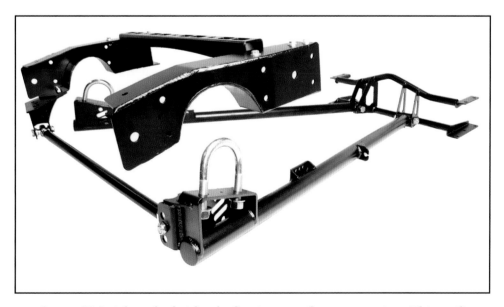

1963-72 GM pickups had either leaf spring or coil rear suspension. This trailing arm upgrade kit from Ridetech offers less unsprung weight, superior control and nicer looks than the factory arms.

The '39 Buick installation detailed earlier uses the original trailing arms after being boxed for strength. Then their front is mounted using standard hot rod urethane 4 bar ends and a simple plate bolted into the X member. Given their mounting on the car centerline the car suspension can easily articulate for road holding, functioning much like the trailing arms seen on 1960-87 GM pickups and many race cars.

The First Gen Corvette had a traction problem as power continued to increase. Engineers came up with a simple expedient answer - by adding an upper bar that makes the front half of the leaf spring act as the lower bar of a 4 bar system.

have fallen out of favor. The problem is that the ladder bar is mounted rigidly to the axle housing in order to control pinion rise, and the forward end pivot is mounted to a bracket on the frame up front. They are heavy and tend to hang low but the real problem has to do with a lack of compliance to road irregularities. When the forward end is split to the outside frame rails they restrict rotation of the suspension when only one wheel hits a bump. You may remember this roll resistance problem from our discussion of split front wishbones on a solid front axle. That roll resistance basically turns the rear axle housing into a giant anti-sway bar. Welds are torn, ladder bars twist and mounting bolts break until the entire structure is beefed up so much to avoid failures so that it becomes massively heavy, delivering neither good ride, handling or traction. And as we discussed in the four-bar section, by changing the angle of the bars as viewed from the side, what is essentially an adjustable length ladder bar is created without the weight and roll stiffness problems. Unless you are building a vintage Gasser reproduction, there simply is no real reason to use ladders bars anymore.

Tractions bars of the slapper type were used often in the 1960s Muscle car era. They mount rigidly to the axle housing, typically under the leaf spring axle pad, and then have a rubber bumpstop mounted in front. As axle wind up and pinion ride occurred the forward bumpstop would contact the spring eye to counter that rotation. These worked fairly well but hang pretty low and do nothing to assist handling.

An interesting evolution of that slapper design and the old Traction Master under-leaf bars has come up in the New Millennium. After mounting the rear of a bar rigidly to the bottom of the axle like the slapper bar, the forward end is mounted to a bellcrank that pivots on the forward spring perch bolt. When the nose of the rear axle tries to rise under acceleration the bar pushes forward and the bell crank rotates in a way that a third bushing contacts the top of the main leaf. This plants the suspension, prevents spring wrap up and controls pinion rise all in one neat package. This is one of the very best traction aids for leaf-spring suspension, and a really neat and simple way to control traction control with no negative effect on handling.

Finally, parallel rear leaf springs can be made to operate much like a four-bar. The GM engineers made a very clever mod to the '59-'62 Corvettes that added an upper bar to that system. The front half of the leaf spring acts as the lower bar, with the back half only taking vehicle weight rather than acting as axle pinion control. With the extra bar to absorb energy, axle wind up is eliminated. We have added similar upper bars to a number of hot rod rear leaf systems with much success. The "three-link" using a single long upper bar near the chassis centerline and a Panhard bar is a variation of this type that can work well if you have the space in the driveshaft area of the floor.

Going back to the whole discussion concerning the importance of a level bar controlling a rear axle, we can extend that concept to leaf springs. The point where the axle housing connects to the spring, or a lowering block, is connected to its forward bushing center to determine the imaginary line or "bar angle". A highly arched spring with a tall lowering block will produce a steeply angled "bar" - and the roll steer we discussed in chapter two often results, along with major league wheel hop because the axle has more leverage over the leaf spring. It would be better to de-arch the spring or use a 2" tall maximum block to keep the "bar" more level. The

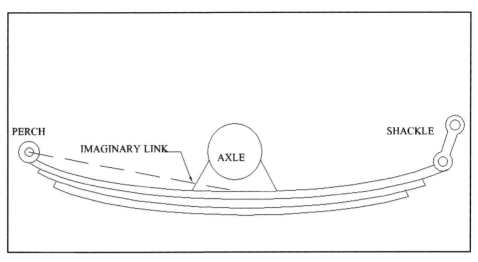

A line connecting the forward spring perch pin to the top of the main leaf spring at the axle saddle mount represents the lower bar of a four bar. Once you understand that, along with the roll steer geometry discussed in chapter 2 and you will quickly see that dearched leaf springs will handle and accept torque far better than a high arch spring with a tall lowering block.

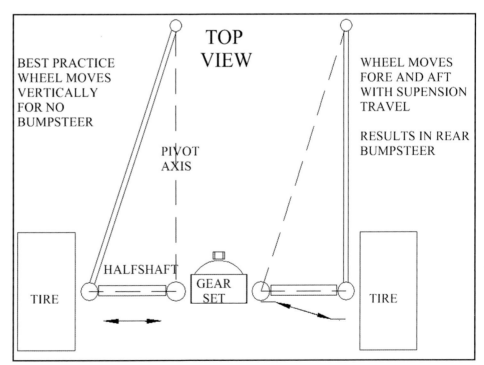

By having the forward pivot of the radius rod in line with the inner pivot of the lower control arm, a right triangle is created. That keeps the tire square in the chassis during suspension travel and avoids rear bumpsteer.

real proof of this is seen on '34-'54 GM cars which originally used a high arch spring. When you jack one up, the axle moves way forward. That makes centering the axle in a hot rod fender more difficult. When the body rolls the axle will appear to move forward on the inside of the turn and to the rear on the outboard side. Now that out-of-square axle will steer the car into a tighter

C-4 Corvette IRS can work very well when properly fit and installed. This installation by Progressive Automotive exhibits the qualities that can make using IRS very attractive.

turn, which we call oversteer. It also illustrates how important this entire level bar/anti-roll steer lecture is to those who think it's not important.

When you have done a bunch of cars and found out what works well, it makes a person appreciate the aftermarket kits more than ever. Most manufacturers have really done their homework on proper design. They wouldn't survive long in the market without good word of mouth advertising. Different designs exist for different purposes, fit up and space limitations and opinions. Collect the catalogs, check the websites, and talk first hand to the vendors at the next show to find the system that suits you best!

INDEPENDENT REAR SUSPENSION

Independent Rear Suspension (IRS) can have some real advantages. The main thought is that handling and ride quality should improve through the reduction of unsprung weight. By separating the action of one wheel from its partner on the other side we should see those improvements in handling and ride quality.. When power and tire traction are taken to high levels and every millisecond counts as in racing, IRS is commonly used when race rules allow or a "World Class" chassis design is intended. In the real world of street driven hot rods, it is the opinion of this writer that very little is gained in a functional sense. Certainly trick appearance and technical complexity are enhanced, but at considerable cost and effort. Those are intangibles each rodder will have to consider and balance for his own purposes when planning the next hot rod project.

The key to a successful installation of an IRS is to either follow

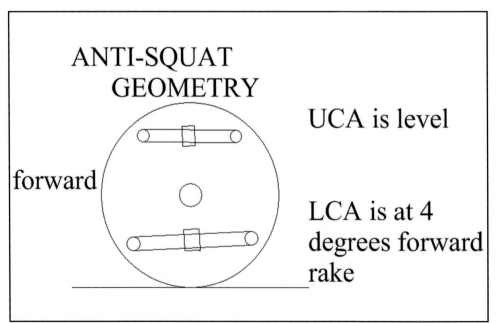

Antisquat geometry prevents weight transfer under acceleration from dropping the rear of the car. Similar to how an inclined upper control arm provides antidive in front, the inclined lower arm causes the antisquat effect in IRS systems.

the aftermarket manufacturer's instructions [if an aftermarket IRS is chosen,] or to carefully duplicate the way an OEM system is mounted. Similar to our discussions about four-bars, when the individual hub carriers of an IRS are located by bar systems it is important to pay attention to arc length theory again. Simply mounting short bars to the frame will cause rear toe in change which will have all the difficulties associated with IFS bumpsteer. A better way is to mount your locating bars so that their inner pivots line up with the inner pivots of the lower control arms of the IRS. That way a right triangle is created as viewed from overhead and the rear wheels are free to move in compliance with the road, with no fore and aft movement or bumpsteer.

The other main way IRS installers get in trouble has to do with antisquat geometry. The idea is that weight transfer to the rear suspension under acceleration can be minimized by changing the angle of the IRS lower control arm (LCA) as viewed from the side. Remembering our discussion of IFS antidive geometry from Chapter Two, that angle of the LCA will be higher in the front while the upper control arms (UCA) remains level. It is interesting to note that antisquat geometry is essentially a mirror image of antidive as used in front. When Jaguar IRS was very popular the four-degree antisquat angle built into the LCA was eliminated by angling the upper differential mount to compensate. This well-meant effort turned out to be dead wrong, done because the antisquat concept was unfamiliar to those early pioneers of hot rod fabrication. Today

we can do better with deeper understandings of good chassis design.

The various Corvette IRS designs from '63-'67, '68-83 (C2 and C3), '84-'96 (C4), '97-'04 (C5), '05-'13 (C6) and '14 up (C7) have all found their way into hot rodding over the years. There are many running changes in their design

The very intricacy of an uncaged Jaguar IRS creates a mechanical marvel that is mesmerizing when fully exposed. It's hard to beat for a T bucket or Model A, but don't expect it to accept 600 HP gracefully.

Another interesting OEM IRS that has seen some acceptance is the T-Bird version from the 1990s. Although it has an odd 4 ¼" bolt pattern, the rest is easily installed in its original cradle. It can be uncaged but replacing the cast aluminum lower control arms with tubular versions is a challenge.

over the years, especially with the addition of a rear mounted tie rod in the C4 to better control toe in changes as power came on and off. Changing from the C2 steel parallel spring thru a fiberglass replacement and then finally coil springs has been able to produce improved ride quality. It is best to carefully measure the mounting points and angles on an original chassis which are then duplicated on new bracketry on the new chassis. Or, one can purchase mounting kits that hopefully have accurately done that work for you.

High standards of ride and handling are expected, although considering the fairly heavy Corvette weight the OEM spring may be too strong for lighter hot rods. That issue can be countered with a replacement spring with a lower rate or a conversion to coil-overs. Although bracketry design can be problematic, conversion to coil-overs offers optimal matching of spring rate to application with attending ride improvement. Another issue to be worked around is that the Vette IRS is designed to fit in a car with a very high rear arch and generally none or very little trunk space. Since most passenger cars and trucks have a much smaller rear rail arch it is often found difficult to get the car ride height low enough without major modification to the frame rails and floor while preserving sufficient travel clearance for the half shafts, hub carriers and shock absorbers.

The Jaguar IRS has seen periods of high acceptance over the history of hot rodding. It has an exceptionally clean style when mounted and looks particularly good when fully exposed as in a T bucket, Model A or pick up. The brakes are fairly small but effective, the real downside can be the fact that it cannot handle large torque and

Here we see the C3 Corvette IRS as enhanced by the VanSteel company. Their years of experience has produced a line of parts that will maximize style and function on a stock Corvette or the IRS installed in a hot rod.

VanSteel

traction numbers very well due to a small ring gear and U-joints. The same frame clearance issues exist as for the Corvette IRS just discussed, but ride and handling are also quite good when set up correctly and with properly matched coil-over rates. The later sedan rear IRS systems are especially popular in pickups as they already use a 4-3/4 on 5 inch wheel pattern like most Chevy cars (Jag roadsters had knock off hubs that need to be reworked in most cases). They are also about 60" hub to hub, which works well in most trucks, although narrowing a Jag IRS is not all that hard to accomplish.

IRS Option

The aftermarket has responded to the call for IFS systems with adjustable width for different applications coupled with the ability to accept wide tires and big horsepower. The Roadster Shop version more than fits the bill with advanced geometry in a pre-engineered package.

Aftermarket IRS designs typically meet all the challenges for which OEM IRS systems fall short in one way or another. By starting with a clean sheet of paper design the goals of strength, handling ability, variable track width, ease of installation and sheer technical attraction are all met. Most use the popular 9" Ford type gearset with all its aftermarket support for ratios and traction assist. Heavy duty U-joints connect the halfshafts to the hub carriers, with upgraded disc brakes a natural part of the package. Radius rod systems are arranged for good geometry and fit in popular hot rod chassis. These sophisticated designs come at a price far more than a simple 9" rear axle on 4 bar and coil-overs, but for the right car and owner, nothing else will do.

This Model A exhibits the Vette IFS in all it's chrome plated glory. This well done installation features an anti-sway mounted in front out of view to control the body roll resulting from the car's high center of gravity and low roll center of the Vette IRS.

VanSteel

Chapter Seven

Hot Rod Springs

Not so Simple as they Seem

Any suspension system must incorporate some way of supporting the vehicle weight as well as assist in soaking up reactions to the natural undulations of the road surface. As this book deals with street driven hot rods we are concerned with paved roads. Now that definition may seem obvious, but it really does help us understand the function of what we will generally call springs. We have previously discussed the geometry of suspensions and now will discuss

A well thought out IFS design will use the aspects of spring mounting in a way that produces premium quality ride and handling. Counter to the thinking of many, good ride and good handling can be enjoyed in the same design when best practices are followed.

the use and purposes of the springs, shock absorbers and sway bars used to allow that suspension to function as planned. We will discuss each of those in their turn as we progress. It's easier to understand each component if you separate their functions.

To begin, if insufficient space is provided for the required suspension travel, that suspension essentially ceases to exist. For a real street driven hot rod two inches of compression and two of extension should be the bare minimum considered, more is always better, especially on the compression side. When a suspension is either bottomed or topped out, travel stops, at that point the spring rate actually goes to infinity. You can easily imagine that this instantaneous halt of suspension travel raises havoc with the ride and handling qualities of the vehicle. It stops being a hot rod and becomes an over powered go cart. The engineer or fabricator's job is to provide enough travel for the suspension to operate, while selecting and mounting springs with the right weight capacity and rate to support the total vehicle weight.

STEEL, FIBERGLASS, OR AIR

Those springs may be leaf or coil made from steel or fiberglass, torsions bars, or air-springs made with rubber bladders. It's really a matter of simple physics. As our discussion of suspension geometry, springs, shocks and sway bars continues, it should become clear that we need a certain amount of force to support a certain weight, and that which type of spring is providing that resisting force really makes very little difference in ride or handling, when the spring is properly chosen and installed. Used wrongly, any spring cannot provide satisfactory service.

If your springs are supporting the car weight at the design ride height while the car is at rest, the springs are correctly chosen and doing all that is required. Some rodders think that a car that bottoms out in a bump it needs stiffer springs, but that approach only works by having a spring rate so high that ride and handling (abbreviated R&H as we continue) are compro-

Different springs can be used in the same suspension to support differing weights due to the engine used and the bodystyle weight. The important thing is to know how to make the proper choice.

The Shockwave by Ridetech offers infinite ride height and spring rate adjustment through varying the internal air pressure. If you need to park lower than you want to drive the car, or carry a light load one day and a heavy load the next, all the while in a compact and trick appearing package, there simply is no other choice.

This traditional transverse, or "Buggy Spring" arrangement provides a traditional style. Note how the ride is varied by using a spacer over the spring which maintains the proper spring rate, rather than simply adding springs leaves until the suspension becomes far too stiff.

Anti sway bars are used to control chassis roll, and the resulting weight transfer in a turn. That helps provide control of understeer versus oversteer in the chassis.

mised. If the spring has some working resistance such as the friction between layers of a leaf spring, there will be some assistance in controlling motion as that weight moves while supported by the spring. However that is truly the job of the shock absorbers.

Again, our understanding of the function of shocks will be advanced of we more clearly understand what they do. In fact they would be better described as dampers in the fashion of our British friends. Rather than try to change 100 years of poor misidentification, we'll just go along and call them "shocks." Truly, the function of shocks is to dampen or control the motion of the suspension. This has become increasingly true as more sophisticated shock technology has allowed ever greater tuning of suspension motion. Today the shock is the brains of the suspension. Therefore we will devote an entire later chapter to nothing but shocks.

Sway bars are another victim of unfortunate naming. All too often that misnomer leads rodders to confuse them with lateral control devices such as the Panhard bar, which do truly control chassis side-to-side sway. Calling them anti-sway bars would be more accurate but the really definitive description would be anti-roll bars as their real function is to control body and chassis sway relative to the road surface. That body roll compared to the road surface has the effect of moving the suspension mounting points away from their previously designed positions which were based on the assumption of the chassis remaining level.

You may recall the discussion of that phenomenon in Chapter Two where we looked at roll steer due to body roll. The other direct purpose of a sway bar is to tune the front to rear weight transfer bias to correct either understeer or oversteer, we will devote an entire later chapter to these very important devices.

LEAF SPRINGS

For now, let's begin our discussion of hot rod springs with leaf springs. Leaf spring suspensions have been in use since the first carriage builder thought he could improve ride quality on his buckboard wagons. It's no surprise that the first cars used an extension of that technology. Many other systems such as coil springs, torsion bars, and Air Ride have been developed to provide various advantages, but it's still hard to beat the leaf spring for a simple, clean way to provide suspension and axle control.

The simplest system was Ford's transverse, or "buggy spring" used from 1906 to 1948. It is very

The earliest Fords used a transverse single spring, often called buggy spring. Great attention must be paid to the details in lubrication and mounting to get acceptable ride quality.

A good example of parallel leafs from a Chassis Engineering leaf spring kit installed on a '40 Ford. By replacing the original single transverse leaf, axle control with a more modern rear axle is achieved, along with properly installed shocks and sway bar to achieve a surprisingly capable suspension.

rugged and saves weight, but requires a torque tube or radius rods to locate the axle fore and aft, as well as in rotation. Ford used the same basic system front and rear. When used with the original unsplit wishbone, the axle is free to rotate about the driveshaft axis, allowing easy travel over the rough roads of the day. On mod-

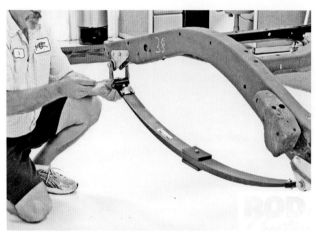

Fiberglass mono leaf springs are gaining in acceptance, offering less weight and noise in operation. With the early production durability issues resolved this may be an viable alternative to steel springs.

ern, smoother roads, the ride quality often suffers due to the fact that a single spring requires a higher rate than two parallel leafs doing the same job. Ride quality can be surprisingly good when the steps we'll mention later are taken to reduce friction between the leaves.

Later GM, Ford, and Mopar cars used a dual spring parallel leaf system. They are found in both front and rear suspensions. This type is very common for street rods today, both updating the original system as well as complete modern kits. The major advantage is their simplicity. The spring controls both axle rotation and position, and only needs locating help with extreme use due to high horsepower engines and sticky tires. Traction bars of different types and Panhard bars are often used to supplement the positioning ability of the leaf springs themselves. Good handling results as the leaves themselves resist body roll, and can easily accept sway bars for more roll control. We discussed those supplemental control devices in Chapter 6, regarding Rear Suspension.

Leaf springs work particularly well in larger, heavier cars with a variable load. By that I mean sedans and panels where the load may be the driver alone one day and four people with luggage the next. We actually prefer rear leafs on most fat fender sedans, coupes and panels with their load carrying capacity. The leaf spring naturally has a variable rate spring in both multi and mono leaf styles. As the spring is deflected, the spring rate increases, giving the ability to carry heavier loads without bottoming.

The tunability of a multi leaf spring can be a

A Posies rear leaf kit is installed in this 1940 Ford new chassis. Inside the rail forward mounting of the leaf springs gives us a low ride without seeing the spring perch under the runningboard. Shocks mounted with lots of travel combine with a rear anti-sway bar for exemplary ride and handling while the narrow spring position allows use of fat tires.

real advantage with our hot rods. Mono leafs and fiberglass springs are very attractive due to their easy action with no internal friction, but they lose the ability to be fine tuned by adding or subtracting leaves. That opportunity to match a spring to an exact application with

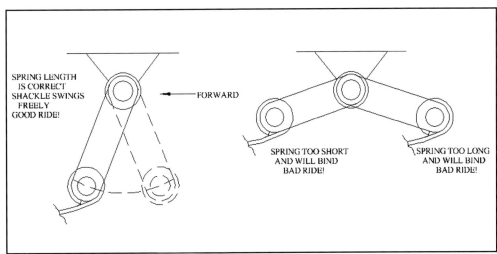

a simple leaf change can be critical with the many variations seen in our cars.

Quarter elliptic springs have found some acceptance in the lighter weight, early street rods where a sprint car style suspension or hidden springing are desired. With a properly braced frame mount that has a spring pre-load device, these can work very well. There will be the need for an axle anti-rotation bar of some type as well as a lateral locator, so they can get more complex than they might seem at first consideration, but this can be an interesting way to fabricate something unique for a car under 2500# total weight range.

How Low Can You Go

It's a simple matter to lower a leaf suspension, provided you have enough axle travel. A spring shop (look in the phone book under truck repair) can reverse the eyes or raise/lower the arch to change the ride height. Aftermarket companies offer a great variety of brand new springs that are already designed to provide a drop. Lowering blocks can be used but should be no more than two inches high. As mentioned earlier, any more

When the shackle is at a 15 degree forward angle the spring is free to change length as it compresses and extends. When the angle is too horizontal, front or rear, the free movement of the spring is restricted with very poor ride being the result.

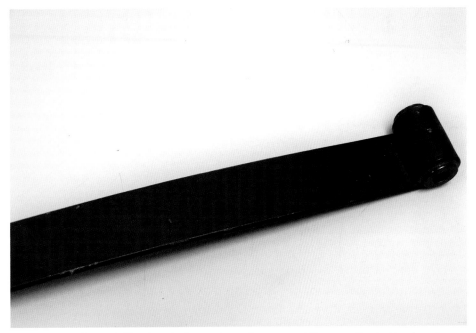

You can make a difficult job far easier when assembling an Early Ford spring, shackles and axle by working with the main leaf alone to get the shackles mounted. That main leaf can be easily compressed to make it long enough to reach the shackles, then adding the rest of the leaves afterwards.

Our earlier photo showed a Shockwave airride unit on this same display chassis, where a simple bolt in swap accomplishes the installation of this coil-over unit. As the coil-over spring is wrapped around a top quality shock, top quality ride and handling will result. Other than looks, the main reason to use a coil-over is the ease of changing springs for a major change in spring rate with fine tuning ride height by adjusting the collar nut under the spring. On this display chassis a lighter than normal spring is used for the unloaded frame. It is normally preferred to have 1"-2" of thread under the adjuster collar.

than that will create access problems to brake adjustment and can cause cornering and wheel hop problems. Blocks do have the advantage of being an easy way to slightly adjust the wheelbase for proper wheel to fender centering. This is really helpful on '37-'48 Chevys and '35-'40 Fords where the fender dimensions are not consistent.

A few simple details make a huge difference in ride quality with leaf springs. First, be absolutely sure that the shock travel neither bottoms or tops out. That is still the major cause of problems in any type of suspension system. Individual leaf spring length must be properly staggered for smooth action. Anything that will reduce the spring's interleaf friction will also pay off in a better ride. The very descriptive term "sticktion" has recently come into use to describe that phenomenon so we'll adopt it here. Aids include Teflon buttons or strips, which are available with molded lips to help keep them in place. The GM cars use a 1 3/4" spring like early Fords, so just get two kits to do both springs. Lubrication is also helpful, and the spring must then be sealed or wrapped with a top quality vinyl tape which will stretch as the spring moves. In fact, most original springs came with a galvanized tin cover. From '35-'48 Ford added a hollow center bolt with a grease fitting and grooved leaves to allow grease to flow between the leaves. Many of these cars have received replacement springs over the years that lack these features, but what a difference they make! Around my shop, the Ford V-8 restorers are always after us to save those original springs for them!

Another very important feature in reducing friction is the configuration of the ends of the leaves. The very best springs have a tapered thickness with a rounded shape at the end. Diamond-cut ends and square cut ends are cheaper to manufacture, but have increased friction at their tips. Teflon buttons or strips will be very important with this style of spring-end.

The tapered style makes an easy transition of load between the leaves for smoother action. This little detail makes an amazing difference in how smoothly the spring works. You can spend the time to grind your spring adding this important detail, or simply buy a spring made that was manufactured this way from the beginning - they look nicer too!

There are also mono leaf steel and fiberglass composite spring available which may save weight while eliminating sticktion. Experience has shown that they do a less capable job of locating the rear axle under acceleration while the integrity of the end fitting on the fiberglass springs has been problematic. The very handy ability of a multi leaf spring to be tuned by changing the number and stagger of the leaves is also lost, so in theory monoleafs are harder to match to our custom built cars. All in all the monoleafs have not gained wide acceptance in hot rodding.

Shackles are required to allow the spring to change length as it flattens under compression. It is important that the loaded shackle angle be about 15 degrees from vertical, leaned toward

The same '55-'57 Chevy chassis also features coil-over suspension in the rear. The adjustable spring and shock tension properties allow fine tuning the finished car to the drivers exact needs. Not only does this look better than stock leaf springs, it will ride and handle far better.

the fixed end of the spring. The length change of the spring is then accommodated by the horizontal swing of the shackle. If the shackle is too near horizontal at ride height, it will restrict the spring travel and hurt ride quality. When that happens, the shackle has to rotate in a vertical mode, and the car will actually have to lift to allow the length change. You can easily imagine how that will hurt ride quality. When the shackle is too long it can hit the perch, again making the spring act like a solid bar. This advice applies to parallel leafs, as well as transverse Ford leafs. It's another good argument for using adjustable perches on a Ford dropped axle; allowing the shackle angle to be adjusted without changing the spring.

Speaking of dealing with length change, too many rodders struggle needlessly with mounting their transverse spring on dropped axle set ups. The original springs had the eyes on the bottom side, and were stretched enough to allow the shackles to be installed by using either a screw jack or hydraulic mechanism. Reversed eye springs don't allow that, and it's really hard to compress the spring enough to get enough length to engage the shackles. A better way is to disassemble the spring and mount just the main leaf to the shackles. The main leaf is easily compressed, and the rest of leaves can be added afterward by use of a temporary, extra-long center bolt, and a pair of C clamps to compress the spring stack. When it's all in place, replace the temporary bolt with the original center bolt. This is an old and simple trick that seems to need relearning. In fact, we often mockup a chassis with a reduced spring pack so that we can approximate final ride height with a car not yet fully loaded.

Some early cars like Buicks and Packards use parallel leafs with a shackle on each end, since a torque tube was used to locate the rearend. We like to make a solid front perch on the stock spring, and retain those springs when adding a late rear end, shocks, and sway bar. If the original springs are in good shape, I'm a big fan of using the springs that you already own. They're already mounted, and designed for the car. We have excellent success with repurposing original leaf springs on cars ranging from 1929 Chevys to 1949 Cadillacs!

All in all, parallel-leaf suspension makes a simple, affordable, and easy to tune suspension

It is common practice, and perfectly acceptable to trim a coil spring to alter the finished ride height. First, be sure ALL 100% of the cars final weight is in place and that the spring has had a couple days or 50 miles driving to settle in. Do NOT think you can estimate the final ride height with sand bags or overweight friends standing on the frame....it won't work!

for the vast majority of hot rods. Many kits are available for specific applications, as well as universal kits that a reasonably skilled rodder can adapt to unusual cars. Today's rodder can buy a kit that will install right the first time without experimentation or the help of a spring shop to modify parts, like in the old days. You are buying someone else's experience instead of getting your own the hard way. Hopefully you've learned a few things that will help you select the kit you want. You can get fancier and more adjustable with other options, but sometimes "simplicity is still the ultimate sophistication".

COIL SPRINGS

The primary advantages of coil springs is that they have no internal friction (sticktion) as do the multi leaf springs, and that they will fit in a confined space, while not requiring the frame rail to extend past the axle as with conventional parallel leaf springs. They do lack the axle locating capability of the leaf spring so some sort of control such as a four-bar will be required.

When the hot rod suspension company guys get together for shoptalk, we find that the number one tech phone call is still referring to their coil spring selection. We have not yet been able to get rodders to understand that the springs CANNOT be finalized until all the final weight is in place. It is really a frustrating waste of your time to change and trim springs to get the rod to set right, and then later add hundreds of pounds worth of interior, glass, radiator water - you get the

idea. The "two fat buddies standing on the crossmember trick" just isn't a very scientific way of determining what spring your finished car will need. When you see a car with an engine removed for a rebuild, you know it's going to set too high. Why is it so hard to understand that an incomplete rod will do the same?

The better way is to leave the springs out while the project is underway. Put a piece of tube or pipe over the shock absorber shaft, immobilizing the shock at a length which will give you the correct final ride height. This is also an excellent way to be certain you will have sufficient travel without bottoming or topping out the shock. That is the number one cause of bad ride quality. Remember that since the shock is about half way to the wheel, wheel travel will be twice the apparent shock travel, due to that leverage. You should wait until the day you are going to the alignment shop to set up the springs. If you get an incomplete car sitting

Seen on this 55 - 57 Chevy chassis are the shock struts we use in set up and shipping.

right, you get to do the work all over again later on with full, finished weight.

Spring strength can be calculated with a formula reading G times d (to the fourth power), divided by 8 times N times D (to the third power).

"G" is the torsional modulus of spring steel, which is an indication of it's elasticity, and is stated as 11.25 times 10 (to the sixth power). The letter "d" is the wire diameter with which the spring is made. N is the number of free coils that can move. D is the average coil diameter, meaning OD plus ID divided by 2 to get the diameter of the center of the actual wire. We can examine this formula to see how complicated this can be.

Manufacturers can make the same spring by varying the number of free coils, wire diameter, and free height. The same spring, made by dif-ferent shops, or the same shop on different days can look completely different from its "twin"! This makes replacing a spring you cut too much too soon very confusing as you start the process all over again.

Perhaps they are building one spring with a certain wire size and want to switch to another design. They can change the other two factors and keep right on running with the "wrong" wire size. In fact, measuring the wire diameter isn't much help since the wire doesn't stay round as it is coiled. Since the wire diameter is multiplied by a power of 4, a few thousands make a huge difference. I think you are starting to see the problem selecting springs, assuming you've been able to get through all the math.

Back to the real world we live in, experience can be the best teacher. The manufacturer of an aftermarket kit should be able to guide you in

As it is often easier to fine tune a spring ride height with a little trim, be sure to do it with a method that won't alter the spring heat treatment. Experience has shown that a full coil is worth about 2" of drop on nearly every car.

Wm. Longyard

spring selection. See their catalog for that info, or talk to tech support. It seems to work best starting with a spring that's a little too tall and trim it no more than a full coil to fine tune the ride height. Expect the car to settle about an inch as the springs break in.

It is possible to safely trim a coil spring that is too tall. The spring must be cut on an open-wound end, so the flat ground end, or any pig-tailed (reduced diameter) spring end cannot be cut. A cold method such as an abrasive cutoff wheel is best. No torches or plasma cutters as they will change the heat treatment of the steel. Remember that each half coil is worth an inch of ride height on about any common suspension.

You can see by the formula that any more trim will affect the spring rate although the spring's total weight carrying strength is not greatly affected. If your original spring choice

was off too much, you'll have to change to a softer, or stiffer spring depending on which way your first choice missed the mark. The best way to do that is to set the old and new next to each other and compare. As you can see by the discussion of manufacturing above, doing it over the phone is a sure recipe for trouble, especially if you have a used salvage yard spring you don't know much about. Send the wrong spring back to the supplier so they can see where you are, and get them to help you make the change to the correct spring.

GM subframe installations can be even more trouble. The springs are difficult to install, and most subframe installations involve an engine setback of from 3 to 5 inches. That has a large effect on weight distribution, combined with the fact that most hot rods have less front-end weight bias than the donor vehicle to begin

Springs on GM subframes are quite large and can be difficult to remove and replace. Since its often hard to find a spring soft enough when that subframe is under a street rod with the engine setback reducing front end weight, a coil-over conversion can be quite useful with broader rate selection, not to mention being far easier to install.

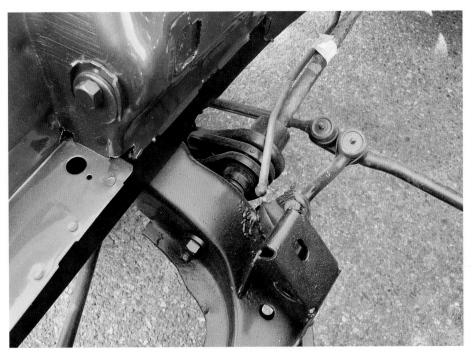

The forward end of the torsion bar has a hexagonal hole in the lower control arm to support this 68 Roadrunner. That requires very strong mounting of the lower control arm to carry the weight and torsional stresses.

The rear end of the torsion bar has another hexagonal recess so a tool can be inserted for preloading that torsion bar. Again, very strong mounting is necessary.

with. A small block installation usually needs a lighter spring than is even available. The change in leverage caused by narrowed control arms and lighter aluminum engine parts changes the spring rate requirement as well. To top all this off, my experience has been that replacement springs seem to always be stiffer than necessary. I suppose they think we're replacing springs that have sagged and that we want a stiffer set.

The difficulties we have discussed lead us to coil-overs and Air Ride. The fact is that these provide an easier way to get the correct spring weight. They come at a price but offer advantages that may make them worth it to you. Mustang suspension is easy enough to work with and correct-rate springs are easily obtained - but that's not always the case with other systems or subframes. Excessively cut springs are the source of most ride complaints, especially with GM type subframes. Coil-overs can be had with nearly any spring rate, and Air Ride is variable for whatever you need. Remember that all the springs do is hold up the car's weight. If it sits right at rest, but you have ride problems, the shocks (the English describe them better as dampers) are likely the culprit. That's our next chapter.

TORSION BARS

Continuing in our discussion of springs, it is useful to think of a coil spring

GM and MII conversion coil-overs offer far better shock control, better spring rate selection and cleaner appearance than separate springs and shocks.

Now we see the plate inserted through the slot in the lower control arm. The plate is tapped for a bolt which is unseen inside the control arm shape, and is turned in or out to hold the preset rotation of the torsion bar and allow fine tuning of the final ride height.

as a torsion bar wound in a circle to save space. Note that the equation for spring force uses the torsional modulus of spring steel. The use of a torsion bar can be a neat way to hide the suspension component inside or alongside the frame rail for a clean appearance. You can also vary the ride height without changing the spring rate as with a coil-over, but without having the coil-over and its mount sticking up from the frame. The frame anchor for the torsion bar must be very strong as there is a lot of leverage involved, while the forward end must have a shackle or a roller device so as not to bind with suspension travel. In some cases the bar is fixed to a well enhanced lower control arm and then has the other end mounted in a frame pivot mount with a jackscrew to adjust ride height. OEM torsion bars are difficult to adapt to lighter weight cars but the racing aftermarket has multiple suppliers who can dial in proper bar spring rates for any car, along with having helpful bracketry for designing your own system.

COIL-OVERS

By mounting a load bearing spring directly on a shock absorber, the coil-over was created.

The use of coil-over suspension units requires a good supply of different springs to match different load requirements. Your supplier can usually get you very close to the right rate based on his experience.

Adding an adjustable lower spring mount makes it possible to fine tune final ride height to the ideal dimension, based on the suspension design, and without affecting the spring rate. Different style ends are available with the urethane-bushed type being generally preferred on the street for NVH (Noise, Vibration, Harshness) suppression. Spherical rod end bushings are often found as well, but generally mounted in urethane rather than the more precise and durable, albeit more noisy, steel outer races.

Coil-overs work best with a load that doesn't vary much, as in small coupes and pickups, front suspensions, and race cars. Bigger cars with varying loads can benefit from the use of variable rate springs. Variable rate springs for coil-overs are created by manufacturing a spring with the coils more closely wound on one end than the other. The end with the more openly wound coils is softer and will compress over the softer bumps while the rest of the spring with the tighter coils is relatively more stiff. That stiffer end won't compress until you hit the bigger bumps or add to the weight loading.

A '34 Ford sedan, for example, really likes a 185/300# variable rate spring to ride well loaded or empty. The first inch of

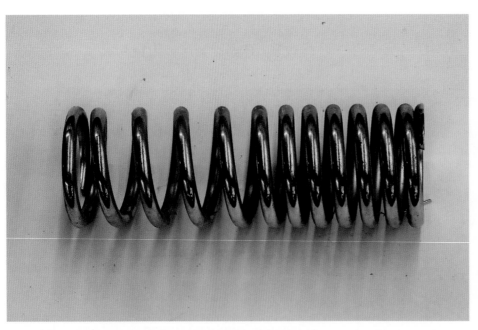

Changing the number of turns per inch on a coil spring has the effect of offering a softer rate at first bounce, and an increasingly stiff rate as the more open wound section approaches the coil density of the closer wound end. This can help the spring handle variable load - why its found on minivans and SUVs today.

travel, over small bumps, will be reacting to a 185# per inch rate for a good ride. Greater weight can then be carried as the 300# per inch rate comes into play to avoid bottoming out.

Some coil-overs (and Shockwaves) feature an adjustable-rate shock, which is extremely helpful in tuning ride and handling qualities. You may find your car heavily loaded or riding on rough roads. You can simply pull over and turn the shock rate knob up a couple clicks. That will dampen the spring motion and prevent bottoming the shock. Running out of travel in extension or compression WILL damage your shocks and mountings. If you are running the new Autocross events, just dial up the shock rate to tighten the handling, and dial it back down for a cushy ride home. Single adjustable units control oil flow both ways, while double adjustable units let the real technophiles among

us adjust compression and rebound individually. We'll get into shocks in detail in the next chapter.

Coil-overs really make the designer and fabricator's job much easier. It is generally a simple matter of mocking up the mounting bracketry given the shock stroke limits and the designed ride height. Then, after the car is weighed it's a relatively simple job to ascertain the ideal spring rate [desired]. The total weight carrying ability of a spring and that spring's rate are related, but different numbers. The necessary spring rate for your project should be available from the manufacturer of your suspension kit, some of the more experienced coil-over suppliers, or by calculation based on the actual measured or seriously-estimated weights.

As most popular coil-overs have a 4" stroke and use a 9" free length unloaded spring, we'll

We'll use the ever popular '69 Camaro in our discussion of how to select a spring rate and the factors that affect that final rate. Calculations will get you in the ball park while experience and adjustability provides the final dialed in rate and height.

SPRING RATE CORRECTION FOR ANGLE MOUNTING

Spring rate correction factors for shock mounting angles measured in degrees.

Shock Angle	Correction Factor
10°	.96
15°	.93
20°	.88
25°	.82
30°	.75
35°	.66
40°	.59
45°	.50

30°

This Trigonometry based diagram will help you see the affect that shock angle has on spring rate and shock function. You will see that a vertical mounting is typically best whenever practical, and how to alter your component choices when mountings require an angle off vertical.

use those numbers for an example of how to find the coil-over rate you need. If the car weighs 3200# and has solid axles front and rear with 50% front weight distribution, and if each coil-over is mounted vertically it would have to support 800# which is 25% of the total weight. Since real cars seldom have a 50/50 front to rear weight distribution, we now have to account for that. Let's say we are working on a '69 Camaro with an LS Chevy engine. That should come out at a roughly 60/40 front biased front end weight, changing the front corner weight to 960# and the rear to 640#.

The accepted formula for the spring RATE is obtained by dividing that 960# front corner weight by the spring free length, then dividing by 25% for a street car, giving us a 427# rate per inch. That means that every 427# of additional load will compress the front spring 1". Using the same formula provides a 285# rate for the rear coil-overs.

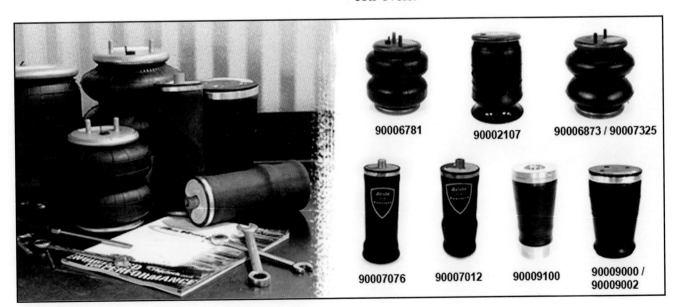

90006781   90002107   90006873 / 90007325

90007076   90007012   90009100   90009000 / 90009002

Airsprings MUST be mounted at an installed height specific to that particular part number. That assures that when the car is aired up the spring rate will be where it needs to be whatever the vehicle weight.

Spring Rate=corner weight
Spring free length x .25

The front IFS will have a leverage ratio we'll get to next, but the rear coil-over is still acting directly on the axle. Remembering all the talk about maximizing suspension travel, let's say you were able to engineer the rear mounts to accept a 5" stroke shock that mounts a 12" spring. Running the same numbers now gives us a 213# rate per inch. Since ride height and weight have remained the same, do you think that the same exact car with a 25% lighter spring rate will ride and handle better? You bet, and the brackets and bolts have reduced stress as well. Does this help you see why maximizing travel is ALWAYS a good thing?

Now let's deal with the two "if's" in our example. First, coil-overs (or any shocks) are often mounted on an angle. High school trigonometry suggests that as a spring is leaned at an angle away from dead vertical, it has to travel further in its own actual length. Translated into spring rate that means that a leaned spring has to be stronger to provide the same rate and carry the same weight as if it were vertical. Back to our example, an angle of as little as 15 degrees carries a divisor of .93. That brings our 285# per inch rear coil-over spring up to 306# per inch.

A well thought out IFS design will use the aspects of spring mounting in a way that produces premium quality ride and handling. Counter to the thinking of many, good ride and good handling can be enjoyed in the same design when best practices are followed.

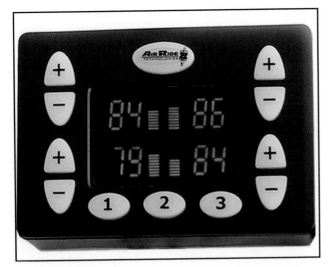

Digital control allows the Airride compressor system to have three preset pressure levels that provide dumped, driving and raised ride heights. It also paves the data road for the auto ride height option.

Again, why lean a coil-over to make it need a stronger spring to do the same job? Sometimes a non fendered IFS may look better with an inclined shock. Taken to the extreme I have seen high end Pro Pick type IFS with shocks at a 45 degree angle. Based on our 427# front coil-over example, that would require an 854# per inch spring! Not on my watch!

Lets deal now with the second "if" in our original example. That issue is control arm ratio. As just mentioned, since an IFS will generally have the coil-over (or really any spring for the purposes of spring rate calculation) mounted on the lower control at some point in between the lower ball joint and the inner pivot bushing. Just for easy figuring let's say the coil-over is mounted on the control arm 65% of the way out to the ball joint, which would effectively increase the necessary spring rate. We divide the 427# rate by .65 and now our '69 Camaro/LS example requires the 427# rate to increase to 656#. Interestingly, experience has shown that a 600-650# rate spring is about right for this application, proving that the science works.

The take away lessons from all those calculations are: weight distribution, mounting angle and leverage ratios all matter. The lighter the

corner weight, the longer the spring, the more vertical the mount and the closer to the point where weight is carried on a control arm - the lighter the spring rate that can be used. Lighter spring rates will always bring less stress on brackets and bolts, better ride, and better handling.

AIR RIDE SPRINGS

I suppose the term Air Ride has become so common in use that, like the Kleenex brand name being applied to all facial tissue, Air Ride has become the common term for air suspension. Full credit for bringing this innovative spring alternative to hot rodding must surely go to Bret Voelkel at Ridetech. We often call the device an "airbag" when the better term is air-spring, so we'll call them that here.

Just as the other types of springs discussed have their advantages, Air Ride does also. When you need to support a variable load on the rear suspension, nothing else works as well as an easily-variable spring rate. At the push of a button, or with automatic control systems, you can maintain that all important suspension travel to avoid bottoming out. That is why they first became common on the working trucks you see on the road. Air-springs are also an easy replacement for a coil spring since you no longer need to attempt to find a replacement with the right height and rate.

The modern hot rodding purpose is more often different. A major part of a hot rod stance is sometimes a really low stance, and there just is not any other form of spring that does that as well. You can have a ride height that has enough suspension travel for safety, comfort and good highway manners, then arrive at a show and drop the car to the ground. When it's time to go home just pump her back up with no more effort than pushing a button.

The very fact that changing the air-spring rate can be accomplished by altering the air pressure makes for good ride quality. No longer do you have to use high rate shorter springs to lower a car. It stands to reason that if the total vehicle weight stays the same but the ride height is cut in half, the decelerating force (spring rate) has to double to do the job. With Air Ride the rate stays essentially the same regardless of ride height.

The number one problem with airspring use comes from a pure lack of reading the instructions. It is absolutely essential that the installer pays strict attention to the published installed height, and ensures that height is maintained with the vehicle mocked up at normal driving ride height. Then, whatever air pressure is required to get to that installed air-spring height will be the correct spring rate for that vehicle. It really is that elegantly simple. It follows that when the weight changes, the air pressure is changed to maintain the planned ride height. That is why an Air Ride system with ride height sensors and digital control is the ultimate way to control an air suspension.

The big difference between the old air shocks and modern air-springs is the volume of air involved. The old air-shocks had very little volume with little space for the captive air to be further compressed, causing a harsh ride. The modern air-spring has a higher volume of air that supports the weight yet still allows the captive air room to compress and maintaining ride quality. Some handling enhancement will come from the lower spring rate of the air-spring, just as we discussed in the section on coil-overs. The real improvement in handling comes when the air-spring is wrapped around a truly premium advanced shock, just as it would with any type spring. Air Ride does add an additional layer of complexity and cost to your hot rod project, but if you want to carry loads or put her down low at the show, there simply is no replacement for Air Ride.

It's hard to believe that with the push of a button this '40 Ford can be raised back up and driven home after the show. This extreme stance isn't to everyone's taste but if this your goal, there simply is no real replacement for air suspension!

Chapter Eight

Hot Rod Shock Absorbers

Really - They're Dampers

Let's get a basic problem out of the way before we begin. Unfortunately we have used the wrong name for what we call "shocks" here in America and our understanding of the function of shocks will be advanced if we more clearly understand what they do. In fact they would be better described as dampers in the fashion of our British friends. Rather than try to change 100 years of poor misidentification, we'll just go along and call them "shocks". Truly, the function of shocks is to dampen or control the motion of the suspension. This has become increasingly true as more sophis-

This highboy roadster exhibits excellent execution of the mounting with plenty of travel, strong mounts and an angle close enough to vertical to give good control. You can believe this is a good driver!

ticated shock technology has allowed ever greater tuning of suspension motion. Today the shock is the brains of the suspension.

Strange as it may seem, the earliest cars were not equipped with shock absorbers. With low speeds and primitive roads the first designers just followed horse drawn coach practice with different forms of elliptic springs. Little thought was given to the need to dampen suspension travel until cars began shaking themselves apart. The first really popular shocks were accessories for the Model T. Some were really just an add-on beehive coil spring to control the original shackle travel, and some were the friction type where a lever attached to the suspension tried to turn against several layers of leather and steel discs. Not too effective but a good beginning on the problem of controlling the suspension.

Next to come along were various forms of lever shocks, often made by the Houdaille company, which has been pronounced 20 ways, the correct being "Hoo-day". The Houdaille version has a rotary paddle inside which forces oil thru a controlled orifice to dampen the suspension. It is interesting to know that Ford used them from the Model A

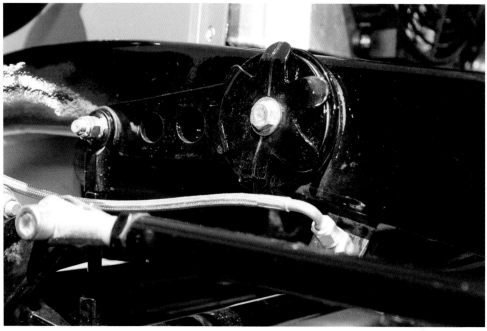

Friction shocks were the first to be seen on early cars and as such have a place on a build theme intended to evoke that more primitive style. The main problems are fast wear and the fact that the resistance is as stiff for the first bit of movement as for the last, which leads to a rougher ride than a tube shock which has a progressive rate nature.

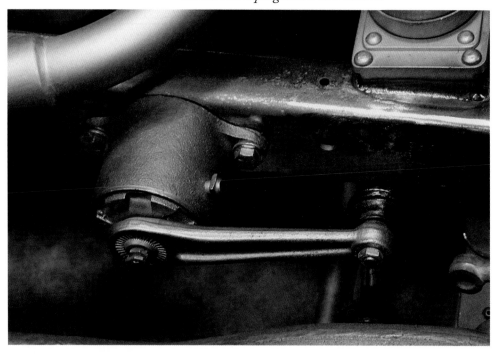

The rotary hydraulic shock is a development of the rotary friction shock in the previous photo. Primarily produced by the Houdaille (pronounced "Hoo-day) company, these provided a better ride with the fluid passing through orifices, thus resisting rotation of the lever attached to the suspension. They are a bear to get apart for rebuild!

109

to 1941, and so did Maserati and Ferrari in the 1940s-1960s! The other main type used on many cars for an upper control arm pivot, rear axle shock or all around on British sports cars, also has a lever connected to the suspension. This design has a piston, connected to the lever inside a housing, which pumps oil back and forth in that cylinder, again thru a metering orifice.

Both type shocks can be rebuilt to work reasonably well, but that rebuilding is quite expensive. Fluids of various viscosities, or an adjustment screw on the Armstrong type, can be used to control the dampening effect but the real problem is that relatively little motion takes place at the rotary paddle or internal piston compared to suspension travel. That high motion ratio means that they have to be pretty darn stiff to accomplish much work.

These shocks certainly have their place in restoration or a project seeking a vintage style. The lever type or even the friction shocks are a favorite on a vintage sprint car build as nothing

else says nostalgia any better. And they work pretty well on the lighter weight cars. But for real performance, with the possible exception of the Armstrongs, they got left far behind when the tubular shock showed up.

Landing gear made with wood and rubber bungee cords sufficed for the earliest airplanes, but as planes got larger and heavier something sturdier became necessary. An extendable strut made with a concentric outer tube and inner shaft was developed and is still used today. That device is known as an oleo strut as it is filled with oil driven thru multiple orifices by a piston attached to that inner shaft, the weight being supported by a Nitrogen charged upper chamber. If you think that sounds just like a modern tube shock, you are correct. In fact, for many years these were referred to as airplane shocks in hot rod magazines. MOPAR led the charge with this type shock, using it on their cars beginning in the 1930s. For some odd reason they chose to mount the shocks between the upper and lower control arms from 1938 to 1951, when they finally moved the upper shock mount to the frame so that they would actually do something!

Shock absorber manufacturers then downsized the strut into a shock absorber and were able to make the whole assembly lighter and less expensive since on a car the springs carry vehicle weight and the shock only has to dampen that spring motion. Gas charged shocks will add a very little to the spring rate since they are hard to compress by hand, but the effect is not considered in the calculations for a street driven car.

The design of traditional shocks is described as twin-tube since the outer body of the shock serves only as a reser-

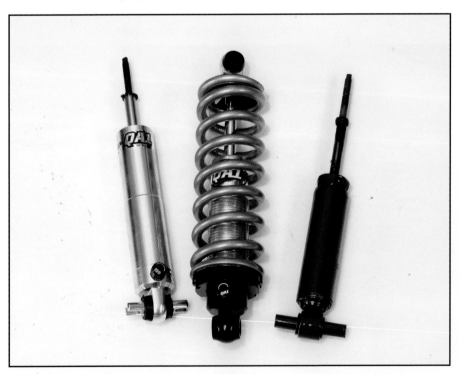

A normal quality blue painted gas is the type you see most often, but the monotube billet shock on the left is the far more advanced option. Internal valving with adjustable resistance is far more sophisticated for improved control AND handling. Add the coil over spring and you have a fully adjustable modern suspension module.

voir for the hydraulic working fluid. There is an inner concentric tube that contains the actual cylinder where the piston is forcing the fluid thru orifices. Many small improvements were made over the years, gas charging being the largest gain, since the gas pressure helped to collapse bubbles in the fluid caused by cavitation as the fluid is forced thru the orifice valving. This type shock must be mounted with the reservoir at the bottom so that the fluid remains in the cylinder. Fluid mixed with air just won't do much in the way of damping, which is the major flaw in the first generation of hydraulic shocks. They did get us from the 1940's up to today, but there has been an entire revolution in shock technology since the 1980s.

This rodder got it all right....the shock arrangement is on the money with travel, angle and strength. The spring shackle angle is correct as well. Although this is shown on an early rod for clarity, the same "rules" should be followed on an installation of any vintage.

MONO TUBE SHOCKS

Racing requirements for better wheel control on faster and heavier cars led to the revolution in shock design. At first the NASCAR racers in particular mounted multiple shocks on the axles and control arms to increase the damping effect. Naturally this was more weight and components than they wished to carry, but design changes were evolutionary until the advent of the monotube shock.

The familiar tubular shape remains, which may be why many rodders have a hard time realizing the immense technical advantages of these shocks, which look the same but cost several times as much as traditional twin tube shocks. A piston

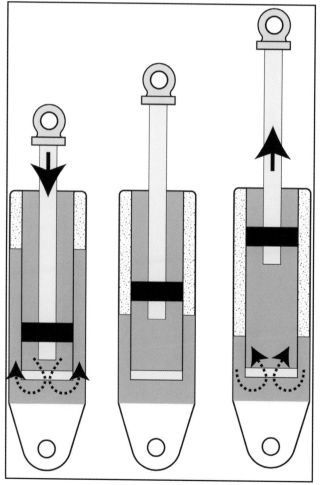

Here you see the traditional dual tube shock cutaway showing its construction. Although OK for light duty, even the OEM manufacturers have seen the benefit of upgrading to monotube designs.

111

Valving the monotube shock has become an art all in itself. Very sophisticated designs provide superb control without harshness. Externally controllable valving has become almost standard and provides the ability to adjust rebound and compression so a shock can be tuned to the particular vehicle. That controllability also allows the driver to stiffen the shocks to play boy racer on the Autocross and then soften them back for a more comfortable ride home. With the advent of electronically adjustable valving and magnetic fluids, those adjustments can be made from inside the car with analog dials.

All that exotic control is wonderful for a competition car where a few hundredths of a second mean a lot, but on the street, a single

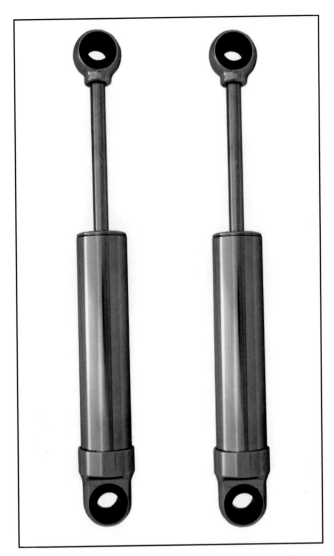

Although the exterior appearance is similar to the traditional shock its internal configuration is an entire technological generation ahead. It's what's inside that counts!

still moves fluid thru valved orifices, but vast improvements in materials and precision machining allows damping control at a level previously unobtainable. The monotube shock allows a larger piston bore so it can move more fluid, meaning an inch of shock travel moves proportionally more fluid, than with earlier shocks, which enhances suspension control. The greater volume of fluid coupled to a nitrogen charged reservoir keeps the fluid cooler and avoids cavitation for more consistent performance. You can even get high-end shocks with external gas charged oil reservoirs for extreme duty.

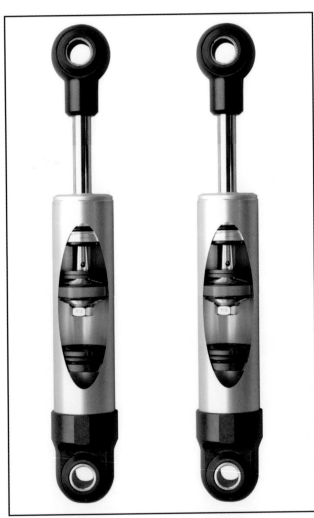

The monotube internal construction shown allows a larger working cylinder for more fluid volume and a larger piston. Those features combine for a cooler running shock with enhanced control.

adjustable shock will perform wonderfully. If you do want to compete once in a while, step up to the double adjustable shock for more control, but spend the time to learn HOW to change the valving. Figuring out whether you want more damping on extension or compression is an art unto itself that can be explored with the double adjustable shock. Misunderstood adjustability can work against you in your chassis tuning. The single adjustable monotube shock will transform the handling of any hot rod with conventional shocks. It comes as a huge shock (pun intended) to many rodders that a so called finished car can achieve a leap forward in handling AND ride comfort with a few hundred dollars spent on advanced technology shocks and a Saturday morning's effort. We have done real world testing replacing perfectly good normal gas shocks with upgraded monotube dampers, and measured G force reduction/ride comfort improvement on the order of 25-30%. And anyone who has watched an autocross event knows what they do for handling.

As was said in the first paragraph of this book, quality handling and ride can be had

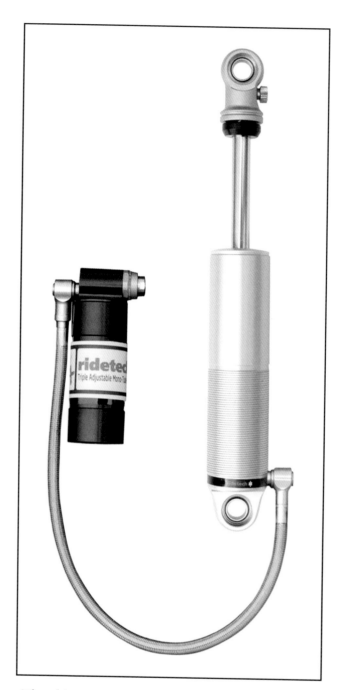

The ultimate iteration of shock technology so far puts an additional fluid reservoir mounted externally with a manually adjusted valve that is far easier to reach than in its usual place on the shock under the car. Cooler working fluid without cavitation are the main performance points.

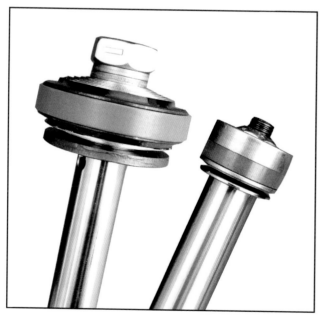

Here is a graphic comparison of the much larger piston in a monotube shock versus the twin tube. It's just like an engine....bigger bore equals the capacity to do more work.

together with the right design, installation, and component choices. Shocks are the brains of your suspension...do yourself a favor and step up to the best!

Chapter Nine

Sway Bars

Suspension Tuning

The best guitar ever made cannot sound right if it isn't tuned properly. A hot rod suspension is really no different. Assuming that a decent basic design was used to build that suspension, it must still be tuned to the taste of the driver and to the purpose for which it will be used. Suspension travel, spring rates, tires etc need to be coordinated. Even less than ideal original suspensions can be improved tremendously with taller spindles for better camber change and tubular control arms with revised geometry. Once the basic system has been

Seeing this Camaro round a corner on track day shows clearly how badly improved camber curve geometry and body roll control are needed. A few simple bolt on parts such as a taller spindle, better shocks and sway bars will totally transform the handling, comfort and safety of this car.

assembled, proper selection of shock absorbers and anti-sway bars can be the easiest and most cost effective way to optimize suspension performance. We've discussed shock absorbers lately, so let's take a look at sway bars this time around.

Much confusion as to the actual function of suspension components comes from the fact that we often use improper terminology. Just as shock absorbers are dampers for suspension travel, rather than absorbing shock, sway bars would be better termed anti-roll bars. Rather than engage in a futile effort to change old habits, we'll call them sway bars for this discussion. They function by resisting body roll, through links that connect the rear axle or IFS control arms to the chassis. The central part of the sway bar acts as a torsion bar so that one side of the body cannot roll (changing its distance to the ground contacted suspension) without twisting that bar. As you can imagine, factors such as bar material, bar diameter, length of the lever end of the sway bar, all will affect the relative stiffness of the anti-sway system.

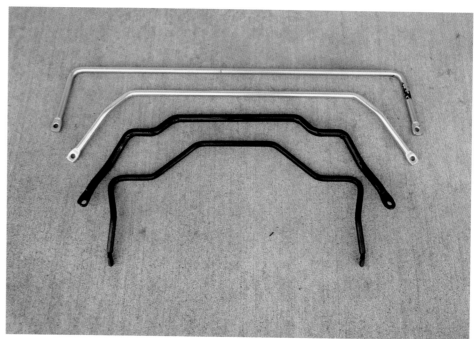

Here are just a few of the sway bars used at Fatman Fabrications. There are many very specific sway bars in both OEM and aftermarket designs with the common characteristic of having unique shapes and lengths to handle the vehicle being assembled.

Wm. Longyard

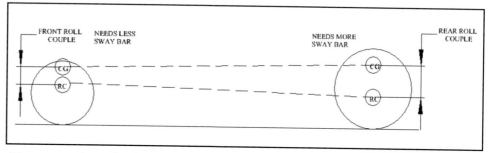

Here we see how the difference between roll center height (RC) and center of gravity height (CG) creates roll couple leverage and causes body roll. When that roll couple is greater on one end than the other, the end with the greater roll couple will need more roll stiffness provided by a sway bar.

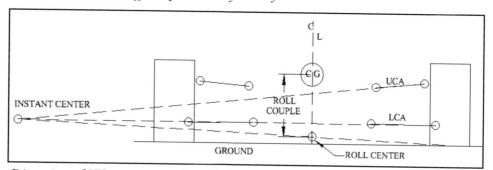

Discussion of IFS geometry explained that a tall spindle/positive caster gain design will lean tires into a corner for better traction and weight transfer. Another advantage (shown) - a higher RC is created with a lower roll couple meaning less need for a heavy sway bar, further enhancing ride quality while maintaining handling ability.

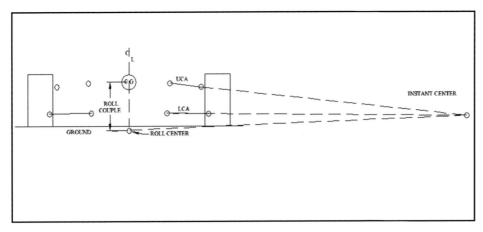

Here the short spindle/negative camber gain IFS design is shown. When the low RC and larger roll couple combines with poor camber gain and CG migration outboard in a turn, the need for a larger sway bar becomes clear. That will lessen ride quality while reducing understeer.

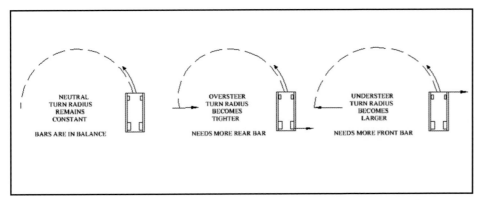

Oversteer is the tendency for the rear to try to turn a tighter corner than the front, the impression that the car is trying to swap ends. Understeer is opposite, the front suspension can't turn as tightly as commanded by the driver and appears to push straight. Roll steer was discussed in the chapter on 4 bars where body roll and poor rear axle control cocks the axle out of square in the chassis, producing more oversteer.

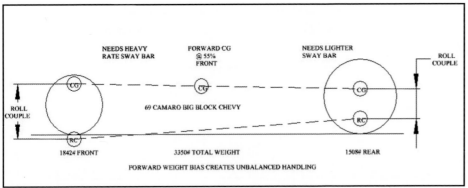

Back to the side view regarding CG, RC and resultant roll couple. This BB nose-heavy muscle car will have a greater roll couple in front resulting in the need for even more front sway bar stiffness. Add increased sway bar requirement due to the negative camber gain geometry common to many of these cars and you have a car that, stock, handles very poorly. This takes us back to why a taller than stock spindle accomplished so much for these cars!

If both wheels on an axle hit a bump at the same time, the sway bar simply rotates in its mounts and should theoretically have little effect on suspension travel. In the real world, bumps in the road tend to be less cooperative than that. Since there will always be some difference in the action of one wheel than the other, it is reasonable to expect that connecting those wheels by adding a sway bar, or increasing the stiffness of an existing bar, will tend to lead to a more harsh ride. That is a good argument for being cautious in adding roll stiffness this way. If the car gets too stiff, the tires will bounce over road irregularities. If the rubber is off the road, it cannot give you traction for turning, stopping, or acceleration.

We want to control body roll because it is uncomfortable for the driver and passengers, while causing a possible loss of tire traction in a turn. When weight transfer occurs during a turn, tires on the outside of the turn can become overloaded while the inside tire becomes ineffective. Suspension design generally assumes that the car stays pretty level in a turn, but body roll acts to move suspension mounting points in regard to the road, thus altering roll centers and messing up what might have originally been a capable design. Poor suspension geometry generally gets much worse when body roll is not controlled, note the nearby photo of the Camaro on the track.

The body roll we are trying to control is caused by the relationship between the cars central of gravity and its geometric roll center. The center of gravity (CG) is the point at which the mass of the vehicle would rotate if you could spin it on a stick. An old rule of thumb says that most front wheel drive cars have a front CG that is about the height of the engine camshaft. The rear CG can be higher or lower based on the design of the car. Pick ups are light in the back and tend to have a low center of gravity while a panel truck CG will be much higher. Connect the front and rear CG, and you find the car's roll axis. It's kind of like having the car on a barbecue spit, turning at those points.

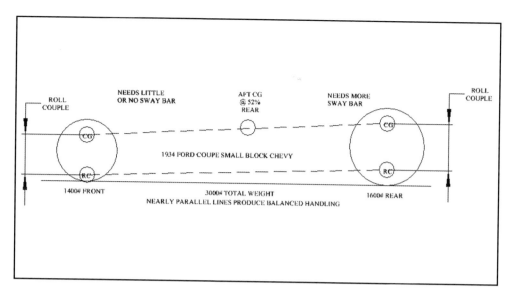

This example of a typical 1934 Ford coupe exhibits almost neutral weight distribution with a rear heavy bias. Since these cars typically will have a positive camber gain design IFS, the roll couple will be relatively small with little body roll or need for a sway the result. However, the slightly greater rear roll couple combined with a relatively high CG makes the addition or a rear sway bar recommended.

Fatman Fabrication's '55-'57 Chevy chassis uses solid sway bars front and rear with urethane bushings for balanced handling and comfortable ride. The rear bar shown stays low to make exhaust routing more easily accomplished.

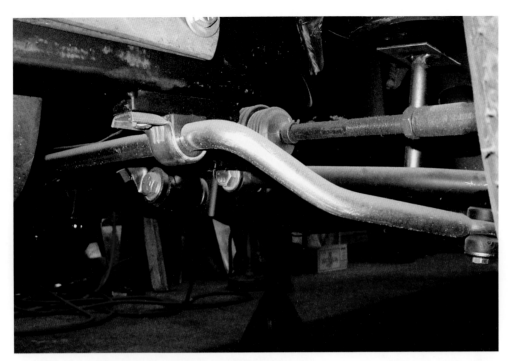

The major advantages of a solid sway bar is a minimal parts count that leads to economical manufacturing, along with the ability to be bent into shapes that take up little space and can snake around other chassis and suspension components.

This rodder chose to retain the factory front sway bar on his '40 Ford chassis. With an IFS swap, a rear bar often provides better balance. I wonder if a restored '40 Ford would handle better with a rear rather than front bar also.

The problem is that the suspension generally has an entirely different idea of where it should rotate. Suspension attachment point locations, ride height, and basic geometry design all serve to alter the geometric point of rotation referred to as its roll center (RC). Again, join the front and rear roll centers and you find the car's roll axis. Using our barbecue analogy, when the RC axis and the CG axis are different, your dinner will flop over as the spit revolves. You've seen that happen. And that is exactly what happens when your car's CG and geometry fight against each other. You can find excellent in depth drawings and discussions of these principles in many suspension books, although we won't go that deep for our purposes here.

A low roll center is often perceived by rodders as being a good thing, but that is generally quite incorrect. It is the difference between the height of the CG and the RC (referred to as the roll couple) that causes body roll. Think of a car running in a circle, attached to a string at the center of the circle. The car CG will be a given height based primarily on it distribution of mass, and actually changes slightly with the speed around that circle. The RC (roll center) is dictated by the height that the string is attached. If the RC is below the CG, the car will roll outward, loading the outboard ties and unloading the inboard. The car also rises a little and the CG moves outboard, making the body roll worse, limited only by the string. In a real car driving in a circle, tire adhesion is eventually exceeded and the car spins out.

If the RC string attach point is above the CG, the car will actually roll toward the inside of the circle. This loads the inside tires and minimizes the outward migration of the CG due to the constant turn. In a real car, you'll go faster with a lot less drama. So, the goal is to use sway bars to control body roll and if possible, raise the roll center enough that a lighter sway bar will do the job. That is one way that good suspension design can also offer superior ride, since a gonzo sway bar that will kill ride quali-

Sway bars have traditionally used a biscuit type end link although that type can be overstressed when suspension travel is large, as with airride. For better control even on OEM vehicles nearly all sway bar pivot and link bushings are urethane today for more precise control, but that less compliant material may actually make high angle linkage more prone to rapid wear.

There are situations where a combination of a spherical rod end is combined with a conventional biscuit type end link bushing to allow more free angle movement without having to change the end on a solid sway bar.

ty need not be used to overcome bad design.

So it all comes down to using sway bars to balance the handling of a car. Just because someone makes a sway bar that will fit your car, or a larger one than it came with, doesn't mean you always want it. If you prefer a nice ride over killer handling, think about using just enough sway bar to control body roll for good handling and passenger comfort. If Autocross is in your future, the game changes. You'll be wanting larger sway bars at the expense of a cushy ride. Most likely, you'll really want to be somewhere in the middle. Rodders have found out that too much rear tire will not allow power to be used to throttle steer the car through turns. Bigger is NOT always better.

As a general rule, the roll stiffness should be increased on the end of the car that is misbehaving. If the car understeers (pushes, in NASCAR speak) add more front sway bar. If it over steers, (loose, as said by the TV race announcers) add rear stiffness. A general rule is that the newer the car, and the larger the engine, the more front sway bar will be required. Engines have moved forward over the years, having the same effect on weight distribution as a heavier engine. We'll use numbers from the QA-1 coil-over company catalog from actual weighed cars for our example. A big block '69 Camaro has about 55% front weight bias and needs a lot more bar than a small block version. And way more than a '34 Ford Coupe with a small block Chevy with 48% front weight distribution. The engine on the '34 probably sits 6 inches further back off the front

The below axle sway bar provides excellent space for over the axle exhaust and stays out of the way when a triangulated rear 4 bar is used. That exhaust clearance is also a big help when you are adding a rear bar to a car that already has had its tailpipes installed..

axle centerline than the Camaro. Since the car's weight distribution and other physical dynamics are so different, you would not want to approach the '34 the same way as the Camaro.

As a point in fact, we just worked on a '34 Plymouth sedan for a customer. He had added sway bars front and rear in an effort to make it handle well, but strong oversteer was the result. The ride was excessively harsh and the driving experience was very "nervous". We removed the front bar, and the car handles much better. The week earlier, we did a '64 Impala for another rodder, adding sway bars at both ends (and fixing some of the factory designed-in bumpsteer) to make for a much improved driving experience.

As a general rule, we run a rear sway bar on everything other than a pick up truck. Panels, sedans, and coupes of all years are included in that list. Front sway bars are used where front end loading increases. Assuming that a small block engine is used, Pre-34 rods seldom need or want a front sway bar, while '55 and later cars nearly always need one. Adding a big block of any flavor, or going to newer cars as the engine mounts get very near the front axle centerline will make a front bar more desirable. On muscle cars in particular, it is generally necessary to increase the rear bar and front bar stiffness together.

Construction ranges from solid bars bent into a shape that integrates the lever arms to tubular type with bolt on or splined levers. The traditional style solid bars are made from high

This Jackie Stewart era Lotus chassis from the Indianapolis 500 has a very slender rear sway bar attached to the lower control arm with spherical rod ends, often mistakenly called "Heim" joints, which is actually a common brand. The over engine mounting keeps the bar out of interference, while later development made the sway bars adjustable from inside the cockpit.

Wm. Longyard

tensile strength alloy SAE 1045 steel, not spring steel as rodders so often think. There are chassis companies that simply bend cold rolled steel bar into a sway bar shape but the ability of cold rolled to not succumb to fatigue would appear to make the alloy steel a better option. Solid construction makes for a bar strong enough for most use in a smaller diameter that will cause less interference with other suspension parts, and no need for multiple parts count. That comes in handy as a solid bar can be bent cold if you have enough power in your shop press, or with heat from a neutral flame torch for a home shop. The manufacturers use heat to make the bends so you can too. The key is to cool the bar as slowly as possible....a bucket of sand or at least an aluminum foil wrap should be used. You really should not weld the bar to widen or narrow it. The variety of OEM and aftermarket bars is endless so if you can't find what you need you can make your own.

Hollow tube sway bars first arrived in race cars in the search for enhanced tunability, and then on muscle cars for a perceived high tech style. There seems to be a thought that a hollow sway bar is lighter, but by the time you add in the extra mass of the bolt-on lever arms it seems that any weight saving is questionable. The principle involved is that the torsional rigidity (modulus being the engineering term) increases at the square of the distance from the tube center. In plain language the material on the outer diameter of the bar contributes more to its rigidity than the material in the center. Imagine how flexible a ½" diameter solid bar would be, and how little is lost by having a 1 ¼" bar with a ½" hollow ID. The racer then can alter the roll resistance (sway bar rate) by changing nothing other than the wall thickness of the bar. Lever ends have to be added, with splined ends being the best but also the most expensive method of attachment. Another acceptable method is a plate welded to the end of the straight tubular bar which in turn has lever ends bolted on. That has to be done with high strength bolts in precisely drilled holes as the shear stress on the bolts is considerable. This method has been proven reliable in practice.

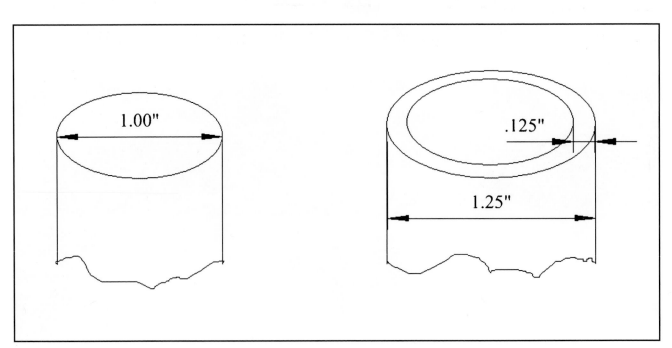

A solid 1" diameter sway has the same resistance to twisting as a 1-1/4" OD x .125 wall tubular bar made with the same alloy steel.

Sway bar pivot and end link bushings were traditionally rubber for compliance but hardly any are today, including the OEMs. As drivers demand tighter handling, urethane bushings have become common practice and will provide minimal compliance yet insulate well enough to avoid being harsh. Many performance oriented sway bars will use spherical rod end links for zero compliance and maximum ability to handle high misalignment angles as the suspension is worked very hard.

Talk to other rodders, as well as the vendors to get good info. Just as you have to do when asking questions in online Forums, you'll soon learn to sort out good info from blather. And when testing your own car, don't be afraid to experiment by temporarily disconnecting sway bar links to see what the effect is. The change, plus or minus, will tell you if you are heading in the right direction. Hopefully, this short discussion will help you wrap your head around what is happening, and pique your interest in learning more. Why drive a car that is less than it could be? Why spend thousands to build it, and then not spend a few hundred to get it right?

This 1966 Chevelle has received the full Ridetech treatment with sway bar, stronger control arms, and coil-over shock and spring conversion. This car will handle and ride as well as any car, including those with IRS. The powder coating of the frame and components provides the detailed touch with minimum maintenance.

Chapter Ten

MII Install

In the Fat Man Shop

We are following along as a '34 Ford receives a Mustang II IFS kit from Fatman Fabrications. Every kit for a different and specific application appears just a little bit different from the others due to the particular frame shape and dimension, but the installation procedure is always the same.

We will begin with the frame set-up. As we've said before - it is NOT necessary to have a perfectly level floor or a surface plate for an

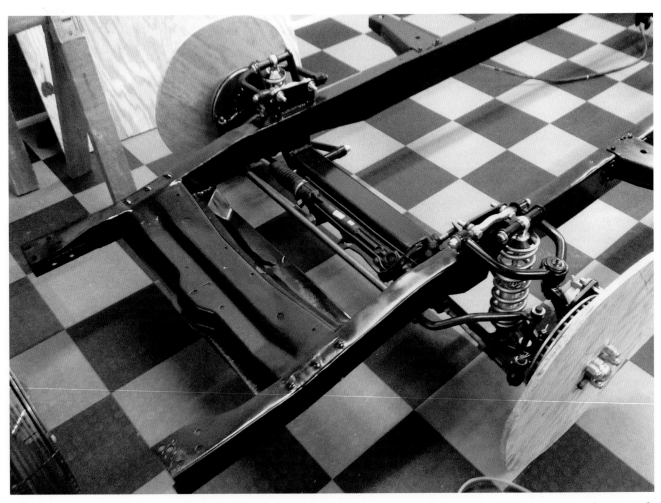

This customer sent a nice photo of his self installed MII IFS kit on a '53-'56 F-100 PU chassis. Note the nice job of boxing the frame while tying that boxing into the stock crossmember for strength. You CAN "try this at home"!

accurate installation. It is the FRAME that must be leveled side to side. Simple sheet steel shims can be tacked to the bottom of the frame rail to accomplish this simple task.

Notice that we do not set the frame level front to back. Since experience has shown that most hot rods of any vintage will have a 2-3 degree forward rake, it makes no sense to do all your careful placement of components in a false level stance. The chapter on four-bars has a detailed explanation of how starting with a leveled frame (the long way) can cause handling problems down the road. Sure, you can make continuous corrections but why confuse yourself.

So follow along as foreman Mike Craig and fabricator Dick Lower follow the logical sub-frame installation sequence. It is the same sequence they've followed many, many times, and the same sequence that is explained in the instruction that come with each of our sub-frame kits.

Note that the level is placed in the "belly" of the frame, about where the center post would be on a 4 door sedan.

Marking the front axle centerline. In this case, you can see the vertical line thru the bolt hole.

This photo shows our Install Shop Foreman Mike Craig and fabricator Dick Lower setting the frame on stands, at the 2-3 degree forward rake we suggest.

We set the frame on a 2-3 degree forward rake. Now we set the new crossmember at zero degrees, cross check for centering, and then finally tack, then weld it in place.

Cross measuring ...

...to center the crossmember.

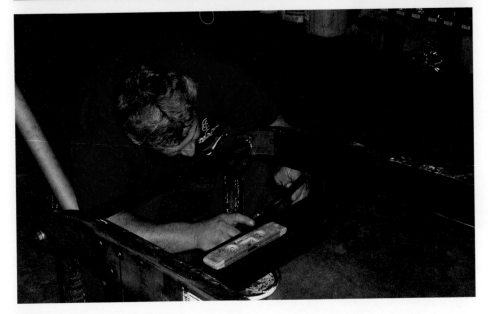

Tack welding the crossmember in place as the complete kit installation continues.

A small yet important point is illustrated by the next photos. The natural inclination of many rodders is to position the shock towers fore and aft by setting the upper shock mount hole directly on the axle centerline.

That is wrong because the upper control arm would then need to be set at a strong angle to move the upper ball joint back far enough to get sufficient caster.

We would rather build in more caster without requiring that upper arm to be so out of square on the mount, or by needing extreme shim stacks when alignment is accomplished. A better practice is to preset a little positive caster by shifting the shock tower just a bit aft, roughly 3/8".

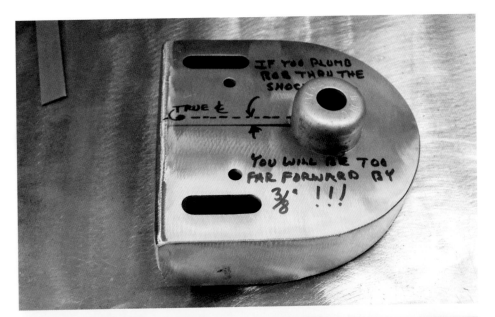

That is why we instruct you to center the inner edge BASELINE of the shock-tower on the axle centerline, knowing that the upper control arm and shock hole will then be shifted 3/8" aft for the desired positive caster.

These photo show a fancier version of the shock tower fixture we use in our own installation shop...

You can do just as well with straight bars tacked or clamped to the shock towers, as suggested in the written instructions.

We are finalizing the shock tower installation with the addition of the gussets.Most other brands of kits have the gussets made as part of the shock tower, which does make the installation a little quicker. We feel that pre-installed gussets also can make the shock tower position inaccurate. The pure fact is that there is more variation in frame rail width from car to car of the same type than you would imagine.

We can also provide a coil-over or Shockwave air ride suspension system for many cars. It is convenient that either uses the same shock tower with a shim system for alignment. The crossmember will be the same as for the conventional spring system just described. Here's a photo of a '34 Ford with that coil-over system installed.

The dimension shown in the top left corner has been left out as it varies with the track width of your kit. For standard width MII kits with a 57" track, that dimension is 36" left to right at the center of the shock mount hole, that dimension being written in as the kit instructions are assembled.

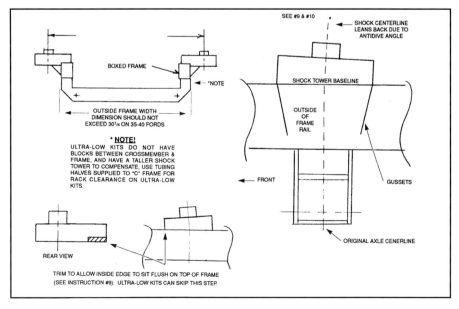

129

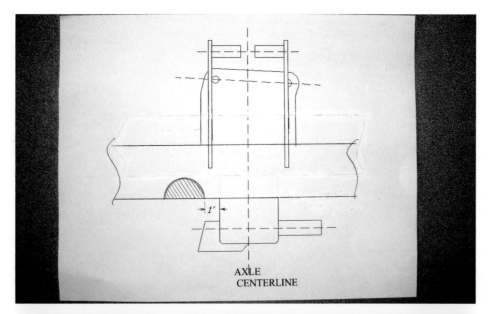

This drawing depicts a coil-over or Shockwave installation. In this side view we are explaining that the coil-over centerline remain vertical and on the axle centerline, while the upper control arm mount (camber plate) has the upper arm moved slightly to the rear to preset some positive caster.

On a standard width MII coil-over installation with a 57" track width, the upper control arm camber plates are mounted at 28" outside left to right. Again, that will vary with the track width of specific kits.

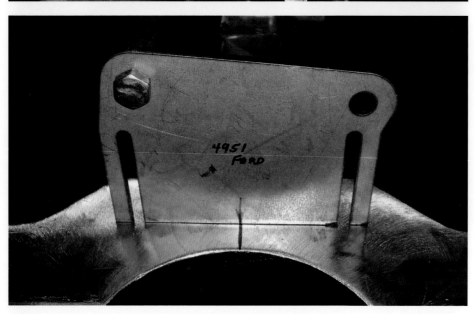

This side view of the upper control arm camber plate verifies that it is mounted with its own base line center matching the axle centerline. Note the upper arm holes shifted rear for some preset positive caster.

As this '49-'51 Ford kit installation is of standard 57" track width, the coil-over side plate mounts are set with the upper bolt centered at 36 ½" left to right.

Since the camber plate is at 28" outside and the coil-over top bolt at 36 ½". One can verify their relationship by checking for this 4 ¼" dimension.

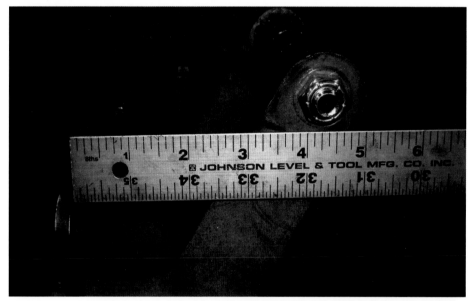

Here is another stand back view of the placement of the camber plate and hoe the preset positive camber is achieved by the rearward placement of the upper control arm holes.

Here we see an overall view of the finished camber plate and coil-over mount assembly. The interlocking tab and slot will provide a very strong mount. IN our shop where we do many installations, we use a 27 ½" long bar tapped for the ½-20 upper arm bolt to make it easy to set up the 28" outer camber plate dimension.

This very important! Although the instructions explain several times that the lower ball joint to control arm junction requires the spacer BELOW the castle nut, many installers miss this step. If the spacer is left on the ball joint stud under the spindle, you cannot get the spindle tight to that tapered stud, and it will feel as though you have a bad ball joint.

Proper installation of the rack and pinion mount bushings requires you to remove the internal steel sleeve from the rubber bushing. Then push the rubber bushing into the rack from the REAR so that the bushing flange will separate the rack from the mounting bracket on the crossmember. Then tap the inner steel sleeve into the bushing. That is FAR easier than trying to install the rubber and steel parts into the rack as an assembly.

It seems we cannot convince installers that the springs cannot provide correct ride height on an incomplete car! Naturally, more weight will compress the spring further, and proper ride height can ONLY be dialed in when the car is 100% complete. To allow setting the car at finished ride height so that the entire build can continue, we supply these short tubes as shock spacers. They convert the shock to a non-compressible strut which holds the car at proper finished ride height.

We have installed the coil springs on this chassis to further explain why springs should not be installed on an incomplete car. The extreme control arm angles and out ward curved springs are the very things that cause panicked rodders to call and tell us they have the wrong spring. For the record, this '39 Chevy chassis sat EXACTLY right with the same springs and with correct level lower control arms - once the COMPLETE car was assembled.

A final step is connecting the rack and pinion to your steering column. Nearly all installations will require 3 U joints with the center mounted to a spherical rod end as a bearing, as on this '69 Camaro.

Chapter Eleven

Fasteners

What we used to call Nuts & Bolts

Bolts and nuts are critical in keeping your hot rod together. Any part that must be assembled and removed periodically will use threaded fasteners rather than a weld or rivet. The wrong choice, or improper installation, can create safety and reliability problems. Different materials, grades, and finishes are available to match the

usage, and the subject of fastener selection and use has filled many a book. The discussion that follows is aimed at providing a few ideas to help you make that proper choice.

There are three basic grades of plain carbon steel bolts that we deal with every day. The Grade 2 bolts have a tensile strength of 74,000 pounds

Fasteners come in a bewildering variety of forms, shapes and specifications. Everything from Grade 8 to no grade at all. Multiple tomes have been written on the seemingly simple topic - consider this a primer. My attempt to make sure you use the best fastener for a particular application.

per square inch, Grade 5 are rated at 120,000psi, and Grade 8 are rated at 150,000 psi. The weakest point on a 3/8" bolt will be at the root of the thread, a diameter of around 5/16", roughly the tap drill diameter. Doing the math tells us that a 3/8" bolt then has .076 square inches under stress. It will theoretically hold a tensile force (one causing elongation) of 5624# in Grade 2: 9,120# in Grade 5; and 11,400# in Grade 8. A common assumption that works pretty well is to assume that the bolt can withstand a shear force (slicing across the bolt) of about 70% of the tensile strength. That reduces the strength in shear to 3936#, 6384#, and 7980#, respectively, so a 3/8" good quality bolt is capable of carrying a considerable load!

Unmarked heads on bolts actually signify Grade 2 common hardware bolt. These should only be used in non-critical strength applications such as fenders and other sheet metal components. Grade 5 bolts have three hash marks on the head, and work very well for general chassis work. The highest tensile strength bolts commonly available are Grade 8, with five or six hash marks. An exception to this is socket, or hex head bolts, which may have flat, button, or cylindrical heads. Many people call these Allen heads (after a major manufacturer), and all are Grade 8, even though not marked as such. Metric bolts will generally have an 8.8 marking on the head, which is roughly the equivalent of a Grade 5 bolt.

In actual fact, Grade 5 bolts are often preferred over Grade 8. A Grade 8 has very high tensile strength, but can be brittle. In applications such as suspensions, a very high number of load/ unload cycles can produce work hardening, which produces an

The most accurate way to determine proper bolt installation on critical areas is using a bolt stretch gauge. Our more familiar torque wrench method indirectly indicates bolt stretch as a function of resistance to turning, but since that is enormously affected by lubrication and technique, values achieved are more averaged than accurate.

A good local hardware can be an excellent source of quality fasteners. Mass marketed discount tool and big box home-improvement stores are notorious for carrying imported fasteners of dubious quality. Fasteners are not a good place to save a few bucks.

135

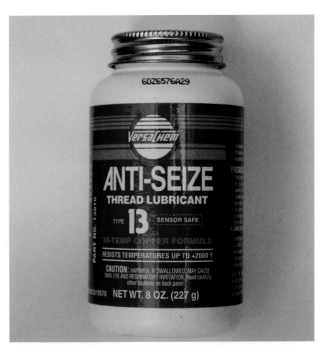

Anti-seize should be used wherever bolt replacement may be a problem, such as a long control arm bolt that fits snugly into a tubular mount. When stainless fasteners are used it is absolutely essential as the stainless fasteners will microscopically weld themselves together. If you and your tools aren't covered with anti-seize residue, you probably didn't use enough!

immediate, or catastrophic failure. It's often much safer to use a Grade 5 bolt which will bend, thus providing a warning, rather than a Grade 8 bolt, breaking without warning. As long as the Grade 5 bolt has been sized large enough to take the expected load, we don't want to trade toughness (resistance to stress cycles) for the ultimate tensile strength of the Grade 8 fastener.

Curiously, I just read a book covering the Titanic tragedy. Being an engineer with a background in Failure Analysis, I was interested to see what had been discovered as to the cause. The prevalent theory today is that the steel held, but the rivets making the seams failed. The technology of that period had begun to introduce steel rivets replacing wrought iron ones. The steel ones have greater strength and are more consistent in quality, but are harder to drive. The wrought iron ones drive easier, had a really good track record in previous use, but were known to have variable metallurgical quality. The Titanic designers therefore used steel rivets for the middle 3/5 of the ship, where stresses were SUPPOSED to be highest (full speed thru an ice field not being normal practice) and the very large hydraulic rivet set tools (10-14 feet tall) could be used. The supposedly less critical stern and bow used the proven, yet possibly variable quality iron rivets, largely because they could be set by men with hammers in smaller spaces.

What we take away from that is that a more brittle material (wrought iron) may have sufficient TENSILE strength, but lacks the ductility to provide the more critical characteristic of TOUGHNESS. Toughness, in metallurgical terms, means the ability to endure repeated stress cycles without failure. For a hot

Pros and cons of stainless. There are special alloys of stainless steel that can be used on suspension parts but they will not be readily available in the hardware store. Confine your use of stainless to non- critical items such as body fasteners and you will be fine........remember to use lots of anti-seize!

rod, I believe that means that a Grade 5 bolt has the tensile strength to do the job without risking the brittleness attendant to the higher tensile strength of a Grade 8 bolt. For a permanently torqued cylinder head bolt, Grade 8 is the way to go, but with suspension stress cycles, I am convinced that a Grade 5 bolt is the better choice.

Bringing a bolt to a torque specification works by stretching the bolt until it gets to a tension force level known as its yield strength. That means that additional tensile stress will not stretch the bolt further, causing it to loosen. If a torque rating is specified, you also need to know whether it is listed as being with dry, or lubricated fasteners. You may have noticed that really critical applications such connecting rod bolts are often set to torque by actually measuring the stretch. Proper torque also helps a bolt resist fatigue failure in an area with a high number of load cycles. Most of the time, on chassis components, fenders, and general use, just tighten the bolts with common length wrenches and ratchets. The length of these are actually calculated to provide proper torque with normal human strength. That's why your wrenches get longer as they get bigger! Don't get carried away and damage bolts by overdoing it.

Based on experience and education, I'd recommend Grade 5 for anything other than engine bolts. Stainless is just dandy for fenders and engine brackets where the trick appearance is worth the expense. Special higher strength stainless bolts are available from the better hot rod fastener specialists for use on applications such as suspension and engine intake manifolds, but you had better be

sure your fastener supplier understands how you are using them.

Cylinder head bolts should remain as Grade 8 or better. Whenever stainless steel fasteners are used, liberal use of anti-seize compound is absolutely essential! Grease is NOT an acceptable substitute. Without it, these stainless steel fasteners will actually undergo a microscopic welding process that will render them seized, and completely useless. If you don't have anti-seize all over yourself and your tools, you aren't using enough!

Nuts are normally made from a grade of steel that is equivalent to a Grade 2 bolt. The idea is no allow the nut threads to deform enough so that they closely conform to the mating bolt. Therefore, even regular nuts should not be reused. The thickness of the nut allows enough material under stress that full bolt strength can be developed. Stronger nuts are used as castle nuts with cotter pins, and also in special applications, generally having a flat washer made integral with the

There are many places where a Nyloc nut just looks better than a plain nut and a split lockwasher. Plus, Nylocs have been proven to be more resistant to vibration. The Nyloc company claims they can be reused up to the 3 times, but I wouldn't reuse any unless the application was truly non critical. You need at least 2 full threads showing above the nylon for the nut to hold effectively. When the joint has rotation as part of its function, such as a brake pedal pushrod, a castle nut and cotter pin would be preferred.

nut. Aircraft fasteners are expensive, but use higher strength nuts, if you have a use that seems to require more than normal security.

Nyloc nuts are extremely popular for use on hot rods, as they generally provide a nicer look than a split lock washer. They also work very well when high levels of vibration are expected. Throttle linkages are real good examples of such vibration, and the rotation of the fasteners in the linkage cannot be tolerated well by most other types of locking device. Just be very sure that at least 3 threads extend through the Nylon, or the locking function will not occur. When Nylocs are used with rubber or urethane suspension bushings, resist the temptation to over tighten. Use a flat washer, and turn the nut one turn after the washer stops turning. Never reuse Nyloc nuts, as the locking effect is greatly diminished after the first use. And don't even think about using them near heat! See your fastener supply house, or aircraft supply for an all steel locking nut that can take the heat.

It's important to think a little about how your bolts should be arranged in the joint. A little trick that I first heard of around airplanes is to try to have the bolt heads forward, and up whenever possible. The idea is that the bolt shank will stay in place and provide some security even if the bolt breaks or the nut vibrates loose. And, you'll have fewer problems finding another nut than another bolt.

To keep your Zinc plated Grade 5 bolts looking better, try making a simple mask from cardboard, and then spraying them with a coat of aerosol clear lacquer. This little trick works well on any metal surface, especially when cadmium plated. Air conditioning fittings, gauge sending units, and brake lines would be good examples. A little quick polish with a 3M

TORQUE SPECIFICATIONS

BEFORE DRIVING YOUR VEHICLE, YOU SHOULD CHECK THE TORQUE ON ALL NUTS AND BOLTS IN THE KIT, INCLUDING ANY SLIDER BOLTS ON THE CALIPERS. RE-TORQUE CALIPER BOLTS AFTER 500 MILES. ALL SPECIFICATIONS ARE IN FT-LBS.

BOLT GRADES

	SAE 2	SAE 5	SAE 7	SAE 8
U.S.	SAE 2	SAE 5	SAE 7	SAE 8
Metric	5.8	8.8	9.8	10.9
Steel Type	Low Carbon (soft)	Medium Carbon Heat Treat	Medium Carbon Alloy	Medium Carbon Alloy

SAE	Bolt Grade	2	2	5	5	7	7	8	8	Socket Head Cap Screw	Socket Head Cap Screw
Bolt Dia.	Thread per inch	Dry	Oiled	Dry	Oiled	Dry	Oiled	Dry	Oiled	Dry	Oiled
1/4"	20	4	3	8	6	10	8	12	9	14	11
1/4"	28	6	4	10	7	12	9	14	10	16	13
5/16"	18	9	7	17	13	21	16	25	18	29	23
5/16"	24	12	9	19	14	24	18	29	20	33	26
3/8"	16	16	12	30	23	40	30	45	35	49	39
3/8"	24	22	16	35	25	45	35	50	40	54	44
7/16"	14	24	17	55	35	60	45	70	55	76	61
7/16"	20	34	26	55	40	70	50	80	60	85	68
1/2"	13	38	31	75	55	95	70	110	80	113	90
1/2"	20	52	42	90	65	100	80	120	90	126	100
9/16"	12	52	42	110	80	135	100	150	110	163	130
9/16"	18	71	57	120	90	150	110	170	130	181	144
5/8"	11	98	78	150	110	140	140	220	170	230	184
5/8"	18	115	93	180	130	210	160	240	180	255	204
3/4"	10	157	121	260	200	320	240	380	280	400	320
3/4"	16	180	133	300	220	360	280	420	320	440	350
7/8"	9	210	160	430	320	520	400	600	460	640	510
7/8"	14	230	177	470	360	580	440	660	500	700	560
1"	8	320	240	640	480	800	600	900	680	980	780
1"	12	350	265	710	530	860	666	990	740	1060	845

METRIC	5.8	8.8	9.8	10.9
Bolt Dia.	Oiled	Oiled	Oiled	Oiled
5mm	3.5	5	6	8
6mm	6	9	10.5	12
8mm	15	22	25	32
10mm	29	44	51	62
12mm	51	76	89	111

The torque values indicated by your tool is greatly affected by the use of a good lubricant such as anti-seize. Be sure to refer to this chart to see the difference. For most applications where a bolt stretch gauge cannot be used, these torque have been time tested and can be relied upon when factory values for a particular application are not available.

pad will bring up a nice shine that will last a couple years when sealed with the clear lacquer. We always keep a can of clear around when doing final assembly on a project car.

Another nifty trick for better cosmetic appearance is to use Nylon washers under plain flat washers in order to prevent damage to painted surfaces like fenders. While you are at it, buy flat normal USS flat washers one size under your bolt diameter, for example, using a 5/16" USS flat washers on a 3/8" bolt. They generally will still fit over the bolt, but are tight enough to stay nicely centered. SAE Grade flat washers will fit better as is, but are more expensive and harder to find.

Here's a fastener identification and torque spec chart for use where no spec is published.

FASTENER SCIENCE : FINE THREAD VS COARSE THREAD

We've all noticed that bolts are available in both coarse and fine thread, but have you ever wondered why and where the different types are preferred? Most of us would agree that fine threads have a more high tech appearance, while coarse threads seem a little less so. There are times, however, when coarse threads are preferred as stronger, when the entire joint is considered.

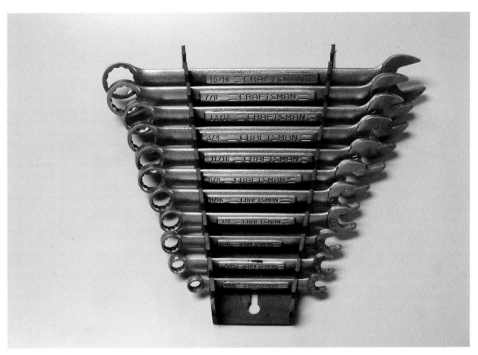

Standard length wrenches are different lengths for a reason. Their length was established as being correct for "normal" (whatever that is) force applied by an adult male to provide the proper torque for that size fastener. Naturally, that ceases to apply when "shorty" wrench sets are used.

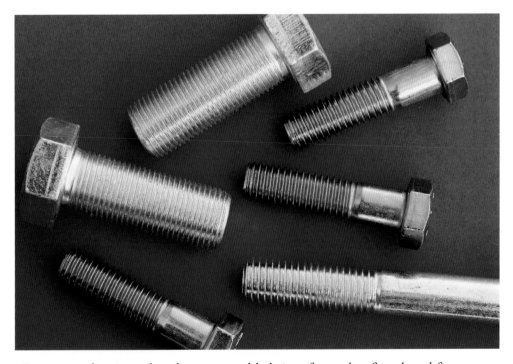

For any application other than a tapped hole in soft metal, a fine thread fastener will always provide a stronger and more vibration resistant joint. Plus, they just appear more professional, since professionals use them wherever possible!

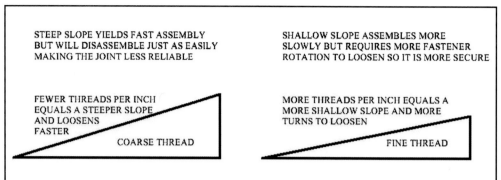

STEEP SLOPE YIELDS FAST ASSEMBLY
BUT WILL DISASSEMBLE JUST AS EASILY
MAKING THE JOINT LESS RELIABLE

SHALLOW SLOPE ASSEMBLES MORE
SLOWLY BUT REQUIRES MORE FASTENER
ROTATION TO LOOSEN SO IT IS MORE SECURE

FEWER THREADS PER INCH
EQUALS A STEEPER SLOPE
AND LOOSENS
FASTER

COARSE THREAD

MORE THREADS PER INCH EQUALS A
MORE SHALLOW SLOPE AND MORE
TURNS TO LOOSEN

FINE THREAD

Coarse vs fine threads Since the coarse thread is like a more steep ramp, a smaller rotation of the fastener produces greater change in the position of that fastener. That is why coarse threads are more susceptible to loosening by vibration.

Before we get into that, let's review some high school physics that will explain why a fine thread fastener can be approximately twice as resistant to vibration and twice as precise in terms of proper applied tightening torque. It all goes back to the inclined plane. An inclined plane is also commonly referred to as a ramp, which is a way to lift a load with less direct force than would be required for a vertical lift of the same weight to the same height. Since there is always a tradeoff between the work accomplished and the motion put into that work, you have to move the weight a greater distance along the ramp, as compared to the height of a direct vertical lift. In other words, for a 1 foot vertical lift, if the ramp allows the one foot rise to be accomplished with a 10 foot long ramp, you would only have to exert a vertical force of 1/10th of that for the direct vertical lift (we are ignoring many factors such as friction for simplicity).

Applying that theory to a bolt tells us that a finer thread is an analogy to a longer ramp since you have to make more turns to move the fastening nut as far as you would with a coarse thread.

That coarse thread can be considered to be a shorter ramp. Taking a common 3/8" bolt as an example shows us that a coarse thread is 16 threads per inch while a fine thread has 24 threads per inch. So, our fine thread "ramp" is 50% longer than our coarse thread example. The nut has to turn 50 % more times to create the same change in its position in terms of distance.

This also gives us more resistance to vibration. Since one turn of the fine thread nut only allows 67% of the

Washers should almost always be used under both ends of a fastener to prevent galling and false torque settings. The availability of different sizes allows better centering on the fastener, especially when space is limited and a larger outside diameter washer will not fit.

length change of the coarse nut (67% is the inverse of the 150% difference in thread pitch, and now we are speaking of LOOSENING the joint). It therefore follows that 50% more turns of the fine thread nut would be required for the same loss of position as would be seen with a coarse thread nut. This is borne out by looking at a torque spec chart, which indeed calls for a higher torque spec for fine threads. Today highly critical bolt torque is expressed in length change under force, again verifying that fine threads are preferable in many cases. For a really good common sense discussion of bolt torque, go online to the Experimental Aviation Association website, and lookup an article by Vance Jaqua, entitled, "Theory of rod bolts and other prestressed bolts".

So, why then are coarse threads used at all anymore? They are less time consuming to produce and are therefore less expensive. They are typically made to looser tolerances, again making them cheaper for use in less critical applications. They will tighten faster, so are more efficient when the vibration resistance and joint strength are less important. One more reason; coarse threads can be a better choice when used in softer materials with less tensile strength.

The strength of a thread is largely developed in the profile of the thread. A coarse thread will leave more material in place between the threads when tapped into a softer material. If we are tapping into cast iron as in an engine block or a soft alloy of aluminum such as an intake manifold, the coarse thread will have that greater material left in the thread root, between each thread. Therefore, since the weak link in the joint is in the tapped material rather than the

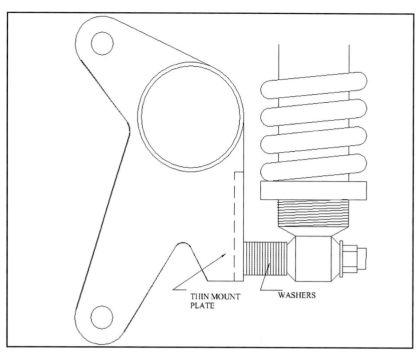

It is very tempting to simply stack washers to make up a spacer when needed. In fact it is a useful way to determine how long a spacer is required, but stacked washers make a weak joint.

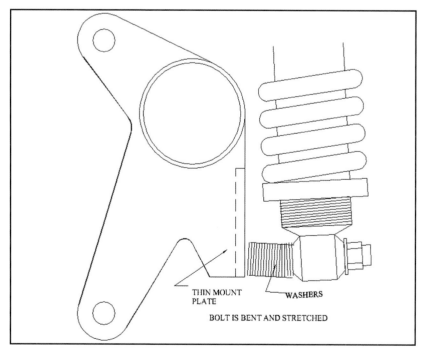

As the washers slide across one another the joint integrity is compromised. The fastener is stressed in both tension and shear, which will lead to early failure as it flexes and work hardens.

bolt or stud, and we have enough joint strength to do the job without needing stronger metal, a coarse thread is a better choice. If you have ever wondered why most studs used on carb mounts on an aluminum manifold have coarse threads on the manifold side, and fine on the nut side, that little mystery has now been solved. We get better thread security in the aluminum with the coarse threads, and better vibration resistance with the fine thread nut on top. And hey, the fine thread still looks more high tech, doesn't it!

We often find it necessary to use some sort of spacer to mount hardware on our hot rods. Coil-over mounting is a common example as the end bushings will be narrower than the diameter of the coil spring, causing a space to be filled on each side of the bushing or bearing. You'll see similar spacing needed on brake pushrod, throttle or shifter linkages. Many suspension designs also use shims/spacers to set the alignment. There are some subtle engineering concepts involved in this question as to whether a couple of washers or a specially made spacer would be better.

It's OK to use plain washers when the needed

space is small and the loads are relatively low. Common hardware store washers are generally of the USS grade. A washer for a ½" bolt will have a 9/16" hole for clearance. We generally buy them one size UNDER so that a 7/16" USS washer will fit snugly on that ½" bolt. Or, as mentioned, you can also buy SAE washers, which fit the bolt diameter much better in their normal size, and have a slightly smaller outside diameter (OD) for a nicer appearance. If you access "Aircraft Spruce" on line you will find a terrific source of specialty fasteners that can be bought in small quantities. Aircraft grade fasteners are all high strength, hardened, and centerless ground for very accurate OD dimensions. Their washers are also available in two outside diameters in all bolt sizes.

You often find it handy to mock up the necessary space thickness with a stack of washers and then machine a spacer to match. If a throttle linkage connecting to an arm on a carb or throttle body with a misalignment less than ¼", a couple washers will do fine given the small distance and light load. A greater space would be better served with either a reshaped arm or a machined spacer with more stability. It really comes down to how the fastener connecting the two parts is supported.

Let's look at a common application with larger loads and distance to make up. A rear coil-over mounting will work well. As you can see in the drawing, the diameter of the coil-over spring requires the shock to be about 1-¾" away from a typical bracket welded onto a rear axle housing. If that distance were made up with a stack of washers, the washers are able to slide over one another, which actually imparts a shear force on the bolt in addition to not providing any real support.

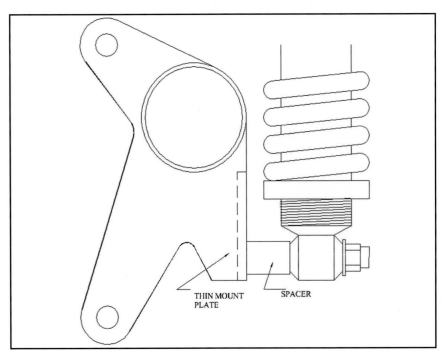

THIN MOUNT PLATE

SPACER

We have now replaced our stack of washers with a proper machined spacer of the same length, but of one piece and squared ends. When a bump is encountered, the joint will be far more secure.

A better approach is to use a machined spacer. Not only will it look better, but the bolt is much better supported. If you think about it, the only way the bolt could be bent would require the spacer to tip on edge. That would impart a tensile load on the bolt rather than the shear load as above. Since shear strength is generally estimated to be 70% of tensile strength, a nice safety factor has been added. Also be sure that the spacer diameter is large enough that the bushing or bearing has its fully covered by the spacer, and has a washer large enough to be sure that the shock cannot come off even if the bushing fails.

To continue improving our mounting design, add a short plate welded to the inside of the axle side of the coil-over mount. A thicker piece of mount material would serve as well, being slightly heavier but easier to fabricate. The final stroke of improvement would be a spacer that not only is one piece, but picks up on an additional bolt hole for an even more secure mount.

We have been looking at a highly loaded example, but remember that the same strength advantages will occur in any application. As a rule of thumb, if the space needed to be filled is over ½ the bolt diameter, I would suggest using a spacer rather than washers. It will be stronger and look more professional. IFS alignment can be established using shims, and those shim stacks measured for height and replaced with a machined spacer. I would still allow about 1/8" for shims to allow a little fine tuning at a later date.

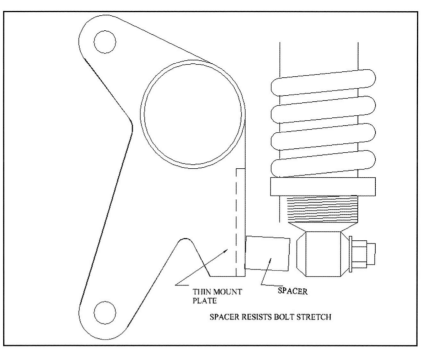

Since the squared end spacer remains perpendicular to the bracketry, the bolt no longer has to endure bending forces. It sees only shear stress and will not fracture by being work hardened thru bending.

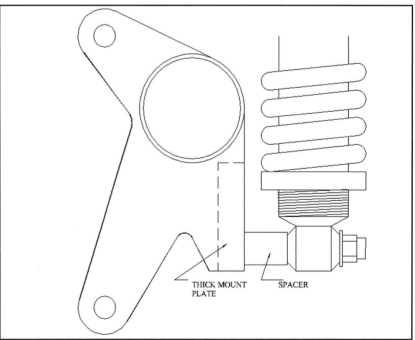

The final improvement of this joint is the addition of a thicker mount at the axle bracket end. Passing that bolt thru a greater thickness further ensures that no bending of the bolt will occur, making the joint even more secure.

Titles	ISBN	Price	# of pages
Advanced Airbrush Art	9781929133208	$27.95	144 pages
Adv Custom MC Assembly & Fabrication	9781929133239	$27.95	144 pages
Adv Custom MC Wiring - REVISED	9781935828761	$27.95	144 pages
Adv Pinstripe Art	9781929133321	$27.95	144 pages
Adv Sheet Metal Fab	9781929133123	$27.95	144 pages
Airbrush How-To with Mickey Harris	9781929133505	$27.95	144 pages
Body Painting	9781929133666	$27.95	144 pages
Building Hot Rods	9781929133437	$27.95	144 pages
Composite Materials 1	9781929133765	$27.95	144 pages
Composite Materials 2	9781929133932	$27.95	144 pages
Composite Materials 3	9781935828662	$27.95	144 pages
Composite Materials Step-by-Step Projects	9781929133369	$27.95	144 pages
Cultura Tattoo Sketchbook	9781935828839	$32.95	284 pages
Custom Bike Building Basics	9781935828624	$24.95	144 pages
Custom MC Fabrication	9781935828792	$27.95	144 pages
H-D Twin Cam, Hop-Up & Rebuild Manual	9781929133-697	$29.95	144 pages
H-D Sportster Hop-Up & Customizing	9781935828952	$27.95	144 pages
H-D Sportser Buell Engine Hop-Up Guide	9781929133093	$24.95	144 pages
How Airbrushes Work	9781929133710	$24.95	144 pages
Honda MC, Enthusiast Guide	9781935828853	$27.95	144 pages
Honda Mini Trail, Enthusiast Guide	9781941064320	$29.95	144 pages
Hot Rod Chassis	9781929133703	$29.95	144 pages
How-To Airbrush, Pinstripe & Goldleaf	9781935828693	$27.95	144 pages
How-To Build Old Skool Bobber - 2nd Edition	9781935828785	$27.95	144 pages
How-To Build a Cheap Chopper	9781929133178	$27.95	144 pages
How-To Build Cafe Racer	9781935828730	$27.95	144 pages
How-To Chop Tops	9781929133499	$24.95	144 pages
How-To Draw Monsters	9781935828914	$27.95	144 pages
How-To Fix American V-Twin	9781929133727	$27.95	144 pages
How-To Paint Tractors & Trucks	9781929133475	$27.95	144 pages
Hot Rod Wiring	9781929133987	$27.95	144 pages
Kosmoski's NEW Kustom Paint Secrets	9781929133833	$27.95	144 pages
Learning the English Wheel	9781935828891	$27.95	144 pages
Pro Pinstripe	9781929133925	$27.95	144 pages
Sheet Metal Bible	9781929133901	$29.95	176 pages
Sheet Metal Fab Basics B&W	9781929133468	$24.95	144 pages
Sheet Metal Fab for Car Builders	9781929133383	$27.95	144 pages
SO-CAL Speed Shop, Hot Rod Chassis	9781935828860	$27.95	144 pages
Tattoo Bible #1	9781929133840	$27.95	144 pages
Tattoo Bible #2	9781929133857	$27.95	144 pages
Tattoo Bible #3	9781935828754	$27.95	144 pages
Tattoo Lettering Bible	9781935828921	$27.95	144 pages
Triumph Restoration - Pre Unit	9781929133635	$29.95	144 pages
Triumph Restoration - Unit 650cc	9781929133420	$29.95	144 pages
Vintage Dirt Bikes - Enthusiast's Guide	9781929133314	$27.95	144 pages
Ultimate Sheet Metal Fab	9780964135895	$24.95	144 pages